'This is a wonderful a
chapters reveal the cru
education. The inspiring and diverse ...
those lessons are drawn from many with their own experience and insight.
It is a vital read for all those who care about autism and education.'
– *Professor Liz Pellicano, Macquarie School of Education, Macquarie University*

'When it comes to autistic pupils, schools are crying out for support. There is no better way to engage support than to listen to and accommodate autistic voices; especially those of autistic teachers and other autistic staff. This book echoes so many necessary and informed experiences, practices and means for real inclusion. It should always be "Nothing about us, without us".'
– *Dr Wenn B. Lawson (PhD)*

'In this wonderful book, autism is allowed to assume its rightful position as an exciting, challenging and enriching element to be celebrated in the diversity of our classrooms. Autistic teachers and school staff have so much to give; this book articulates the difficulties, certainly, but also shares the warmth, the enthusiasm and the humour that an open autism presence brings to our schools. Highly recommended.'
– *Dr Clare Lawrence, Senior Lecturer in Teacher Development and Head of Participatory Autism Research, Bishop Grosseteste University*

'Rebecca Wood brings together stories from the autistic teacher community that will impact conventional autism narratives and cultures of schools. This book challenges lazy or harmful stereotypes about autism, but from the "inside-out", and invites the reader to experience perspectives that are rarely explored, and yet vital to cultural learning and change. It is a landmark publication in recognising the strengths associated with autism in the teaching profession, and mitigating the challenges faced by autistic teachers.'
– *Richard Mills, AT-Autism, The John and Lorna Wing Foundation, University of Bath*

'A highly compelling and original book that is a "must-read" for anyone interested in inclusion and education. Insights gained from the personal narratives and experiences of autistic teachers provide powerful opportunities for discussion and reflection on what truly inclusive environments and practices could, and should, be. Written in a highly accessible and engaging style, this book helpfully challenges the dominant narratives of autism through illustrating inclusive practices and connecting these with current research theories and priorities.'

— *Sarah Parsons, Professor of Autism and Inclusion,*
University of Southampton, UK

'This book provides a wide range of insightful and illuminating perspectives from rarely heard voices: autistic teachers. The authors not only discuss their own personal experiences but give practical suggestions on how to support autistic teachers and how their particular interests can be used to benefit the school. This polyphonic work is hopefully the beginning of a larger and long-overdue discussion of how we can make our schools a more inclusive place for all.'

— *Annelies Verbiest, co-author of* The Everyday
Autism Handbook for Schools

'This excellent anthology of voices from autistic professionals and academics is an immensely valuable read, and one which fills an urgent gap in autism understanding. This book will be a vital tool not just for teaching staff aiming to understand autistic perspectives, but for increasing the expectation within educational fields for the voices of autistic professionals to be heard, valued and learned from.'

— *Chris Bonnello, autistic advocate, author and*
specialist education teacher

'If there is one place where we can start building a more inclusive society, it is at school. It is the children of today who will shape society tomorrow. Of course, this mission can only succeed if today's school itself is inclusive. And it's not just about the students, it's about the teachers as well. Like no other, this book shows the added value of autistic teachers.'

— *Peter Vermeulen, author*

'An essential read for any education leader or professional. It will open your eyes to the benefits of opening your ears and listening to autistic staff members. You, your school, and your learners will be the richer for it.'

— *Charlene Tait, Deputy CEO of Scottish Autism*

'An honest insight into the world of autistic educators, sharing their passion for the profession and showing the true depth of empathy that they have for their students. This book is a valuable resource for all educators, parents and policy makers, as well as autistic people considering a career in education

and those wishing to support their autistic pupils and colleagues. We must nurture our autistic and otherwise neurodivergent educators and recognise their true value not just to autistic students but to the profession as a whole.'
– *Kabie Brook, autistic activist and advocate, co-founder of Autism Rights Group Highland, National Autistic Taskforce Director*

'Finally, a book that harnesses the professional experience and personal insights of autistic educators! *Learning from Autistic Teachers* is a must-read for anyone dedicated to making our schools more inclusive and accessible.'
– *Meghan Ashburn, creator of Not an Autism Mom and That Au-Some Book Club, educational consultant, author and teacher*

'This book offers a rare degree of insight into what autism is, and what it means in a school environment. These autistic educators have seen what autistic children go through in education, from both sides. Schools will always be neurodiverse places, both among the children and the staff; to be truly inclusive, they need to get to grips with what neurodiversity means in practice. The writers here are exceptionally well-placed to help them to do that.'
– *Fergus Murray, autistic teacher and co-founder of Autistic Mutual Aid Society Edinburgh (AMASE)*

'Schools that aim to be informed by the neurodiversity paradigm must engage with neurodiversity amongst school staff as well as pupils. Harnessing the expertise of neurodivergent school staff can promote creative and effective solutions to the challenges of true inclusion. This must-read volume of perspectives from autistic educationalists makes an essential contribution to that effort.'
– *Professor Sue Fletcher-Watson, Professor of Developmental Psychology, University of Edinburgh*

'There are a number of books which focus on how to make a school setting inclusive for students who have been diagnosed with autism. This book focuses on the experiences of autistic teachers where each individual shares their struggles and successes and provides information on what worked for them to be successful teachers. It is also about self-discovery and the importance of understanding autism at a personal level. This is a useful book for anyone who is interested in understanding lived experiences, and for those who are considering of making organisations inclusive for staff with different needs and strengths.'
– *Dr Prithvi Perepa, Lecturer in Autism Studies, University of Birmingham*

of related interest

Inclusive Education for Autistic Children
Helping Children and Young People to Learn and Flourish in the Classroom
Dr Rebecca Wood
Illustrated by Sonny Hallett
Foreword by Dr Wenn B. Lawson
ISBN 978 1 78592 321 0
eISBN 978 1 78450 634 6

Supporting Spectacular Girls
A Practical Guide to Developing Autistic Girls' Wellbeing and Self-Esteem
Helen Clarke
Foreword by Dr Rebecca Wood.
ISBN 978 1 78775 548 2
eISBN 978 1 78775 549 9

The Neurodiverse Workplace
An Employer's Guide to Managing and Working with
Neurodivergent Employees, Clients and Customers
Victoria Honeybourne
ISBN 978 1 78775 033 3
eISBN 978 1 78775 034 0

Our Autistic Lives
Personal Accounts from Autistic Adults Around the World Aged 20 to 70+
Alex Ratcliffe
ISBN 978 1 78592 560 3
eISBN 978 1 78450 953 8

Learning from Autistic Teachers

How to Be a Neurodiversity-Inclusive School

EDITED BY
**Dr Rebecca Wood, with Dr Laura Crane,
Professor Francesca Happé,
Alan Morrison and Dr Ruth Moyse**

Jessica Kingsley Publishers
London and Philadelphia

First published in Great Britain in 2022 by Jessica Kingsley Publishers
An imprint of Hodder & Stoughton Ltd
An Hachette UK Company

1

A CIP catalogue record for this title is available from the
British Library and the Library of Congress

ISBN 978 1 83997 126 6
eISBN 978 1 83997 127 3

Printed and bound in Great Britain by CPI Group

Jessica Kingsley Publishers' policy is to use papers that are natural,
renewable and recyclable products and made from wood grown in
sustainable forests. The logging and manufacturing processes are expected
to conform to the environmental regulations of the country of origin.

Jessica Kingsley Publishers
Carmelite House
50 Victoria Embankment
London EC4Y 0DZ

www.jkp.com

In memory of Dr Dinah Murray,
who taught us much

This book is also dedicated to
Helena Stephenson, Rebecca's
mother, and a lifelong teacher.
To quote one of her favourite sayings:
'If you can read this, thank a teacher!'

Contents

PART 1: UNDERSTANDING AUTISTIC TEACHERS

PART 2: INTERSECTIONALITIES

Autistic School Staff Project

ASSP

Foreword

Dr Laura Crane and Professor Francesca Happé

Most books on autism and education focus on the inclusion of autistic children and young people, and they are written from the perspective of non-autistic professionals. This hugely original volume represents an exciting and significant shift in focus: not only considering the inclusion of autistic school staff but, crucially, prioritising the voices of the real experts on autism – autistic people themselves.

The traditional model in autism research and practice is that non-autistic people analyse, interpret and convey autistic experiences. This book, primarily authored by autistic school staff and curated by a team of autistic and non-autistic editors, is an important step towards shifting this narrative. Contributors provide strikingly honest accounts of the opportunities and challenges that autistic school staff encounter; they challenge myths about autistic people that have pervaded autism research for decades (e.g., that autistic people lack empathy; for counter evidence, see Nicolaidis *et al.* 2019); and they highlight the important and varied contributions that autistic staff can bring to schools – not merely meeting the same standards as non-autistic staff, but bringing something different, and extremely valuable, to their work.

The lead editor of this volume, Dr Rebecca Wood, has conducted truly pioneering research as Principal Investigator of the Autistic School Staff Project,[1] out of which this volume was developed.

---

1   At the time of writing, the Autistic School Staff Team comprises Dr Rebecca Wood, Dr Laura Crane, Professor Francesca Happé, Alan Morrison and Dr Ruth Moyse.

The Autistic School Staff Project, funded initially by the Economic and Social Research Council and subsequently by the John and Lorna Wing Foundation, brings together autistic and non-autistic educationalists and researchers with the aim of facilitating diversity and inclusion in schools, and supporting the equal rights of autistic school staff. Dr Wood has drawn together a brilliant and wide-ranging group of autistic contributors. Across their chapters, they discuss a variety of roles and topics relevant to schools, share their experiences and insights, and offer valuable suggestions and advice.

We were particularly pleased to have the opportunity to be part of this hugely original project, since it aligns very much with topics that we have focused on in our own respective research areas. For example, much of Laura's research has focused on highlighting the stark inequalities that autistic people face when navigating a world designed around non-autistic norms, which can take an extremely negative toll on autistic people's well-being (e.g., Crane *et al.* 2019). Such challenges are frequently noted within the frank and honest accounts provided by the contributors to this volume, at all stages of their career journeys, including when training to be a teacher, working in classrooms or leading a school. Similarly, the unique cognitive style, including eye for detail, that characterises autistic cognition has been the focus of much of Francesca's work (e.g., Happé and Vital 2009). This different way of looking at the world is associated with talent in many areas, including art, maths, memory and music. The skills, dedication and passion that autistic school staff can bring to their work is aptly captured in many of the chapters here.

Several chapters in this volume also relate to other major developments in the autism research field, notably two prominent theoretical accounts from autistic scholars. First is the Double Empathy Problem (Milton 2012; Milton, Heasman and Sheppard 2018). Double Empathy theory outlines how autistic people can often struggle to understand the thoughts, feelings and experiences of non-autistic people but that, critically, the converse is also true. Across several chapters, contributors to this volume discuss the lack of understanding they encounter from their non-autistic peers and school leaders; providing first-hand accounts of the issues that can arise due to a mismatch in neurotype (i.e., whether a person is autistic or not). Identifying ways to facilitate shared understanding across neurotypes will be essential in ensuring that autistic school staff are fully supported in their roles, and the accounts included within this volume represent an important first step towards this goal. Importantly, the concept of Double Empathy may also underpin some of the strengths that autistic school staff bring to the classroom. For example, a growing body of research has documented the successful ways in which autistic people can foster a shared social understanding with one another (e.g., Crompton *et al.* 2020; Heasman and Gillespie 2019). Likewise, a recurring theme throughout this volume is the beneficial way in which autistic school staff can develop a deep sense of empathy and rapport with their autistic students, uniquely understanding their needs. In this regard, the expertise of autistic school staff may be a critical factor in facilitating the educational inclusion of autistic pupils.

A second major theory that pervades this collection of writings is monotropism: the tendency to focus deeply on a single intense interest, to the exclusion of other inputs (see Murray, Lesser and Lawson 2005; Murray 2018). This volume is not the first place where monotropism has been considered in relation to the school context. For example, in a seminal study by Wood (2021), the role and function of intense interests for autistic children in schools was powerfully emphasised. Specifically, Wood suggested that even though monotropism could have some negative consequences for autistic pupils in schools (e.g., lack of engagement with the full curriculum), it could also predominantly afford a range of benefits (e.g., greater independence in their learning). This 'double-edged sword' of monotropism was also apparent in several chapters in this book, with contributors noting the significant pedagogical benefits associated with encouraging autistic school staff to draw on their intense interests within their teaching, but also acknowledging the challenges that may arise if this is not accommodated. The autistic contributors to this volume certainly echo Wood's (2021) recommendation that there needs to be greater consideration of the ways in which monotropism can be incorporated into curricular and pedagogical perspectives; both for the benefits of students and their teachers.

A further important theme emphasised within this volume is the often-neglected topic of intersectionality. Intersectionality refers to how factors such as disability, gender identity, race, ethnicity, cultural heritage and sexual orientation 'do not stand alone, but rather interact (or intersect) in complex ways that affect individual experience, notably to increase marginalisation and discrimination' (Cascio, Weiss and Racine 2021, p.22). Reflections on intersectionality within the field of autism research have cautioned against researchers reducing autistic people to their label or diagnosis while ignoring other important aspects of their identity that shape their lived experience (Cascio *et al.* 2021). Attending to issues of intersectionality therefore represents another key step towards creating more inclusive and supportive school environments for all. The contributors to this volume should be commended for raising this critically important issue, and we hope that their writings mark the start of a much-needed conversation around this topic in autism education.

As we move towards the close of this Foreword, we want to emphasise that our role in authoring this piece is definitely not to 'speak over' the autistic contributors of this volume, but rather to amplify their call for non-autistic professionals to listen to the expertise that autistic people themselves have to offer. In this regard, this volume will be of interest to a diverse range of readers. Autistic people working in schools (in any capacity) can use these first-hand accounts to reflect on their own journeys in the education profession, with aspects of these accounts potentially providing helpful validation of readers' own lived experiences. Autistic school staff may also be able to learn from others who have found effective ways of navigating their careers in education. This may be particularly pertinent since a number of our contributors had somewhat unorthodox routes into an educational career, often due to the inaccessibility of traditional routes into employment within schools. Likewise, non-autistic people working in schools can use this volume to reflect on how to support their autistic colleagues; facilitating greater appreciation of the challenges that colleagues may face in training and employment, as well as recognising and utilising the diverse strengths that autistic colleagues can bring to their roles in school.

We also urge *all* readers to reflect on how this volume can foster an inclusive whole-school ethos, whereby inclusion is promoted and facilitated at every level, for both students and staff. This will involve reflecting on the negative experiences discussed by many contributors, but also considering what works well, in order to develop further existing good practice. We hope that this volume also reminds readers of the immense value of diversity in schools, and the wide-ranging skills that autistic school staff can bring. This book is more than a series of writings about how to thrive as an autistic member of school staff – it also touches on the qualities needed to be a skilled member of the education workforce more generally.

Finally, we express our immense gratitude to Dr Wood for the opportunity to be involved as part of the Autistic School Staff Project team. We are delighted to have the opportunity to write the Foreword for this pioneering volume, which will undoubtedly have a major impact on research, policy and practice regarding the educational inclusion of both autistic staff and students for years to come.

References

Cascio, M.A., Weiss, J.A. and Racine, E. (2021) 'Making autism research inclusive by attending to intersectionality: A review of the research ethics literature.' *Review Journal of Autism and Developmental Disorders, 8*: 22–36. https://doi.org/10.1007/s40489-020-00204-z.

Crane, L., Adams, F., Harper, G., Welch, J. and Pellicano, E. (2019) 'Something needs to change: Mental health experiences of young autistic adults in England.' *Autism, 23*(2): 477–493. https://doi.org/10.1177/1362361318757048.

Crompton, C.J., Ropar, D., Evans-Williams, C.V., Flynn, E.G. and Fletcher-Watson, S. (2020) 'Autistic peer-to-peer information transfer is highly effective.' *Autism, 24*(7): 1704–1712. https://doi.org/10.1177/1362361320919286.

Happé, F. and Vital, P. (2009) 'What aspects of autism predispose to talent?' *Philosophical Transactions of the Royal Society B*, 364: 1369–1375. http://doi.org/10.1098/rstb.2008.0332.

Heasman, B. and Gillespie, A. (2019) 'Neurodivergent intersubjectivity: Distinctive features of how autistic people create shared understanding.' *Autism, 23*(4): 910–921. https://doi.org/10.1177/1362361318785172.

Milton, D.E.M. (2012) 'On the ontological status of autism: The "double empathy problem".' *Disability & Society, 27*(6): 883–887. https://doi.org/10.1080/09687599.2012.710008.

Milton, D.E.M., Heasman, B. and Sheppard, E. (2018) 'Double Empathy.' In F. Volkmar (ed.) *Encyclopedia of Autism Spectrum Disorders*. New York: Springer. https://doi.org/10.1007/978-1-4614-6435-8_102273-1.

Murray, D. (2018) 'Monotropism: An interest-based account of autism.' In F. Volkmar (ed.) *Encyclopedia of Autism Spectrum Disorders*. New York: Springer. https://doi.org/10.1007/978-1-4614-6435-8_102269-1.

Murray, D., Lesser, M. and Lawson, W. (2005) 'Attention, monotropism and the diagnostic criteria for autism.' *Autism, 9*(2): 139–156. https://doi.org/10.1177/1362361305051398.

Nicolaidis, C., Milton, D., Sasson, N.J., Sheppard, E. and Yergeau, M. (2019) 'An expert discussion on autism and empathy.' *Autism in Adulthood, 1*(1): 4–11. https://doi.org/10.1089/aut.2018.29000.cjn.

Wood, R. (2021) 'Autism, intense interests and support in school: From wasted efforts to shared understandings.' *Educational Review, 73*(1): 34–54. https://doi.org/10.1080/00131911.2019.1566213.

Acknowledgements

We would like to thank all of the participants who have contributed so far to the different stages of the Autistic School Staff Project (ASSP) by providing their invaluable expertise and insights. Without them, we would not have been able to develop our understanding of this much under-researched professional group, and take the first tentative steps towards supporting the needs and recognising the strengths of autistic school educators. Our participants have also enabled us to identify the elusive missing link in the inclusive education field: the acknowledgement that we cannot support diversity amongst pupils if we are not doing so for those who teach them.

We would like to thank the John and Lorna Wing Foundation who have generously funded the project on two occasions and enabled this book to be produced within a relatively short space of time. Our work has also been helped by Scottish Autism (SA), through funding and by highlighting our project on their networks: we would especially like to thank Charlene Tait, deputy Chief Executive Officer of SA, for her ongoing support of the ASSP. Autism Rights Group Highland (ARGH), with the particular assistance of Kabie Brook, have made an important contribution to the ASSP by enabling us to recruit a consultative committee at the start of the project in 2019 which, at that stage, was funded by the Economic Social and Research Council under grant number ES/S011161/1.

Other organisations that have helped us to recruit participants are the Pan London Autism Schools Network – Research group; the Participatory Autism Research Collective (via Dr Damian Milton); the Times Educational Supplement; the Scottish Women's Autism Network (via Dr Catriona Stewart OBE) and the National Association of

Head teachers (via Dr Rona Tutt OBE). This process was additionally supported by disability and education specialist, Marguerite Haye, Professor Nick Hodge of Sheffield Hallam University, Dr Georgia Pavlopoulou of University College London and Nicole Whitelaw of the University of Huddersfield. Shagun Agrawal of King's College London kindly provided help on a voluntary basis during her summer break. Francesca, Laura, Rebecca and Ruth have been supported in their work on this project respectively by the Institute of Psychiatry, Psychology and Neuroscience of King's College London, the Centre for Research in Autism and Education of University College London, and the School of Education and Communities of the University of East London.

Disclaimer

The editors of this book consider that it is important to enable the chapter authors to write openly about their experiences and views. It is only by doing so that we can understand the difficulties experienced by autistic school educators, as well as their particular skills, and work towards providing better professional circumstances for neurodivergent school staff. However, the editors were unable, nor was it considered appropriate, to attempt to validate the veracity of the accounts from the chapter authors. Therefore, the editors, their employers and the ASSP funders are unable to take any responsibility for the content of chapters in terms of the experiences described in relation to current or former employers.

Terminology

In this book, we employ 'identity-first' language in relation to autism, for example, 'autistic teachers'; 'autistic children'. This is in response to the overall preference of the autistic community, as far as we can ascertain, for identity-first language (Kenny *et al.* 2016), and the conceptualisation of autism as an inherent part of individual personhood, rather than an element that could (and should) be separated or even removed.

With regard to whether or not to write 'autism' and 'autistic' with or without a capital 'A', we have respected the choices of individual authors in this regard. Similarly, although in this book a deficit narrative is predominantly avoided when discussing autism, there are slight variations in this on the part of individual authors, which we have not sought to homogenise. Other choices of terminology on the part of individual authors have also been retained.

Readers should also be aware that we have not sought a uniform definition of 'neurodiversity' or 'neurotypical'. However, as editors we have found it useful to be cognisant of the description from Kapp (2020, p.2), whereby 'neurodiversity' is understood as 'a broad concept that includes everyone: both neurodivergent people (those with a condition that renders their neurocognitive functioning significantly different from a "normal" range)'. 'Neurotypical', meanwhile, refers to people within a 'socially acceptable range' of neurocognitive functioning (Kapp 2020, p.2).

References

Kapp, S.K. (2020) 'Introduction.' In S.K. Kapp (ed.) *Autistic Community and the Neurodiversity Movement: Stories from the Frontline.* Online: Singapore: Palgrave McMillan. Available at https://link.springer.com/book/10.1007%2F978-981-13-8437-0. (Accessed 01/12/21)

Kenny, L., Hattersley, C., Molins, B., Buckley, C., Povey, C. and Pellicano, E. (2016) 'Which terms should be used to describe autism? Perspectives from the UK autism community.' *Autism* 20(4): 442–462.

Illustration of Learning from Autistic Teachers by Sara Peeters

Introduction

AUTISM AND INCLUSION: HAVE WE BEEN LOOKING IN THE WRONG DIRECTION?

Dr Rebecca Wood

Education is one of those topics on which we all have an opinion. Not least because most of us in the UK went to school, or are parents of children who do or did so, or live near schools and either are, or know, teachers. It also seems to be an area government ministers can't help tinkering with, as each new administration or cabinet reshuffle leads to a raft of policy changes, modifications in funding priorities and alterations to school governance structures. So just in case our minds drift onto other pressing issues of the day, we are constantly drawn back to considerations about exams, inclusion, teachers' pay, the curriculum, behaviour policies and the rest.

In the midst of all of this, children go to school. Parents get them ready in the morning, attend parents' evenings, supervise homework, wash their uniform. But not all children, and not all parents. In fact, although figures vary on this, according to the UK's Department for Education (DfE), children in England with additional support provided by Education, Health and Care Plans (EHCPs) are more than twice as likely to receive permanent exclusions, and more than four times as likely to receive a fixed-period exclusion (or suspension) than children without Special Educational Needs and Disabilities (SEND) (DfE 2020). And these figures don't include children who have been 'off-rolled', that is, removed from the school without the formal exclusion procedures having been undertaken. This is when the removal 'is primarily in the interests of the school rather than in the best interests of the pupil' (DfE 2019), a process thought to impact disproportionately on children with SEND (McShane 2020). So although we all feel we know what 'school' means, and have been talking about 'inclusion', for example, for decades, schools are highly complex institutions, where social inequalities can be both initiated and maintained (Domina, Penner and Penner 2017).

As far as autistic pupils are concerned, the reality is just as troubling. Subject to relatively high levels of formal exclusion, those who attend school may well experience multiple manifestations of 'soft' exclusion, such as part-time attendance, limited contact with the class teacher, a patchy curriculum, and conditional access to after-school clubs and trips (Wood 2019). To add to this assortment of exclusionary ingredients, the sensory and social environment of schools can be overwhelming for many autistic children, making it impossible to concentrate and creating high levels of distress (Ashburner, Ziviani and Rodger 2008). This in turn becomes another exclusionary factor, when autistic children cannot cope with mainstream or even special school environments, and so find themselves unable to attend due to anxiety or overwhelm (Goodall 2018). Even with changes to law, policy and numerous interventions, training programmes and, of course, a substantial body of research, these issues stubbornly perpetuate.

It does seem self-evident that no teacher goes into the education profession intent on ignoring or excluding certain children and, given the current nature of schools, it is debatable whether school staff are provided with the resources, opportunities and framework to make inclusion a reality for all (Allan and Youdell 2017). Not only this, but our conceptualisation of, say, 'a teacher', or 'a teaching assistant', tends to be one-dimensional, even though there are approximately half a million teachers and two hundred and seventy thousand teaching assistants in England (DfE 2021), roughly equivalent to the population of Leeds, one of the largest cities in the UK (Office for National Statistics 2021). Yet despite the sizeable nature of the school workforce, and our enduring preoccupation with the business of schools, we seem to spend relatively little time reflecting on the sheer diversity this personnel must represent. Indeed, while we worry about inclusion for children, and try to figure out how to achieve this, we don't pay much attention to school staff in this regard. We don't consider if their differences are recognised, supported and valued, and whether they feel 'included' in their place of work. We must question, therefore, if it is reasonable to expect this ideal of 'inclusion' to become a reality for children, without taking into account whether it exists for the people who teach them.

This question, along with much-needed preoccupations with the employment rights of disabled people, forms the core of the Autistic School Staff Project, from which this book is drawn. It would seem that despite many years of focusing on the educational experiences of autistic children, their teachers, who might also be autistic, have simply not been considered. In fact, when we looked into it, we found that even though there is a growing body of research into the employment experiences and needs of autistic people, most of it centres on either behaviourally-informed interventions, or office or tech environments (Wood and Happé 2021). Very little indeed takes into account the unique nature of the school workplace and the particular characteristics of teaching and other education roles. In short, we realised that, for many years, as we have been training our sights on autistic pupils, we have simply been looking in the wrong direction. Or at least, we should have been looking the other way too, and considering autistic adults as well as autistic children in schools.

So what did we find? Well, it might be no surprise to learn that according to our research participants, the issues that affect autistic children also impact on autistic school staff. Of the 149 school staff who responded to our initial, UK-wide survey (Wood 2020), many complained that the sensory environment of schools was very difficult to deal with, to the point of being overwhelming. Significantly, this was across different roles, as teachers, teaching assistants, trainee teachers, SENCos (Special Educational Needs Co-Ordinators), senior management, visiting professionals and even head teachers responded to our survey. Crowded corridors, noisy break-times and hot, stuffy classrooms, all meant that the working environment was difficult and tiring, adding to the pressures of a busy job. In addition, social issues, which have long been established as creating difficulties for autistic children in schools (Locke *et al.* 2010), were found to be problematic for autistic staff too. These issues might result from the complexities of school politics, unexpected changes announced from management, or the sheer number of social exchanges that take place during a typical day (Wood and Happé 2021).

Moreover, just as autistic children can experience prejudice in relation to their diagnosis (Aubé *et al.* 2020), some of our participants reported similar difficulties. Overhearing autism discussed in a negative way in their place of work, or having to engage in autism training which was less than enlightened, was hard to deal with. Sometimes the support provided to autistic pupils was felt to be of poor quality, which was not only upsetting but, combined with the prejudiced attitudes about autism they had experienced, meant that participants feared revealing the fact that they were autistic to their colleagues. The same issues arose in the process of training to be a teacher, as trainees felt conflicted over whether or not to be open about their diagnosis and, by extension, ask for the accommodations they needed. As a result, some of our participants ended up hiding or masking their autistic traits, a process that is both stressful and exhausting (Pearson and Rose 2021).

All of these factors combined mean that, according to our study, autistic school staff can experience mental health issues and burnout, resulting perhaps in a reduction of working hours (and so receiving less pay), stepping back from senior roles, not seeking promotion opportunities or even dropping out of the teaching profession altogether. Indeed, a third of our participants were no longer working in the teaching profession at the time of completing the survey, and while a small number had made this change for positive reasons, most felt they had been effectively driven out of the profession (Wood and Happé 2021).

Importantly though, many positives were suggested by our study. These are both heartening in themselves, and also indicative of what needs to be in place to avoid the problems I have outlined. Some participants described good experiences of sharing their autism diagnosis, meaning colleagues respected their views on how best to support autistic pupils, for example. Being open about their diagnosis also meant that they could be a role model for autistic children, as well as their parents, reassuring them that one day, their own child could potentially fulfil a professional role. In addition, while communication with non-autistic colleagues was found to be difficult on occasions, the same did not apply to the pupils, with whom they described a strong rapport and even a bond. This was particularly the case with autistic pupils, who participants empathised with, knowing instinctively how to pitch and pace their teaching. The combination of these factors meant that some participants felt they were making a strong contribution to educational inclusion, especially for autistic children, but also for those with other special educational needs and disabilities.

It was striking too that despite the many difficulties I have summarised, a high degree of satisfaction with the teaching profession was expressed by our participants (Wood 2020). Some participants even used the word "love" to portray their attitude towards their work. Indeed, developing subject specialisms and, by extension, a deep enthusiasm for their work, is not only reminiscent of 'monotropism' (a tendency to develop very strong interests, considered to be a key autistic trait [Murray, Lesser and Lawson 2005]), but suggests too that we should be doing much more to encourage autistic people into the education profession. Furthermore, while unexpected changes were difficult to deal with, especially for teaching assistants, some of our participants felt that the structured nature of the school routine particularly suited autistic teachers.

The next phase of our project, which consisted of 33 in-depth interviews, took place during a particularly unusual and challenging time: the Covid-19 pandemic (Wood *et al.* 2021). As readers can imagine, all of the issues already described became much more complex – throwing up positives and negatives – during lockdown and the work changes resulting from Covid-19 safety measures in the UK. These included, for example, part-time or even full-time home-working for specified periods, social distancing measures in schools and the removal of all but essential items from the classroom.

From a sensory point of view, our interviewees found that working from home was highly beneficial, as was the stripped-back school environment, with classrooms decluttered, gaudy wall displays removed and the usual noises toned down. On the whole, the changes to work practices resulting from the pandemic were found to be better from a social perspective, as participants described reduced numbers of children to deal with, and fewer interactions with staff and parents on a daily basis. These adjustments were felt to help autistic pupils too, who benefitted from working in smaller groups, or 'bubbles', and not having to change for gym classes, for example. However, teaching remotely and especially engaging in meetings via video call were considered to present their own complexities, because social rules are harder to gauge. In addition, the blurring of home/school boundaries was found to be problematic, particularly if participants usually masked their autistic traits at work. Moreover, the sheer number of changes and adjustments required as a result of the pandemic, particularly if these were communicated poorly or at the last minute, were very difficult to deal with.

Our interviewees also asserted that arrangements and accommodations requested in pre-coronavirus times, and rejected as impossible, had become the norm, and even an obligation, during lockdown. These included flexible arrangements for children suffering from school-based anxiety, or remote access for meetings. Overall, therefore, our research suggests that the failure to support and listen to autistic teachers can result in missed opportunities for both staff and pupils, and that their insights ought to be fostered and valued more.

Crucially, the participants in our Autistic School Staff Project worked across mainstream and special school sectors, and included visiting professionals and those in an advisory role for local authorities. Readers will see a similar diversity reflected across the different chapters of this book, signifying that autistic people can and do fulfil a range of roles in the school sector, and that they are already making a strong contribution to the education of our children. Just think how much more they could be doing with the right supports and accommodations in place.

Our study also encourages us to think more deeply about the nuanced intersections between teaching and disability, whereby support and understanding are perceived as bi-directional, rather than founded on a conceptualisation of the disabled person with 'needs' (Neca, Borges and Campos Pinto 2020). This means that teachers with disabilities are recognised as vital members of the workforce, without whom the entire school community would be impoverished. Taking this a step further, our research indicates that we should also re-evaluate notions of the 'teacher expert', and aim for a more relational approach to education. Within such a formulation, learning is perceived as a shared process between pupils and their educators, thus empowering children with special educational needs in particular, as well as their teachers (Ljungblad 2019).

If education is a topic on which we all have a view and is seldom absent from the pages of our newspapers, we must ensure that the public conversation is not partial. When we discuss exams, school uniforms, behaviour policies, the impact of Covid-19, etc., we must be aware of the significant numbers of children who are excluded from our school system and can be ignored in political discourses. Similarly, we need a greater cognisance of the diversity of staff in our schools, in terms of ethnicity, gender and, of course, disability. I suggest that paying greater attention to autistic and other neurodivergent school staff will create a necessary shift in our perceptions of educational inclusion, which remains stubbornly elusive, despite all of our efforts. By understanding and valuing autistic school staff, and providing them with the necessary supports, we not only fulfil our moral and legal obligations towards this neglected workforce, but also lay a path for better futures for autistic children too.

References

Allan, J. and Youdell, D. (2017) 'Ghostings, materialisations and flows in Britain's special educational needs and disability assemblage.' *Discourse: Studies in the Cultural Politics of Education, 38*(1): 70–82.

Ashburner, J., Ziviani, J. and Rodger, S. (2008) 'Sensory processing and classroom emotional, behavioral, and educational outcomes in children with autism spectrum disorder.' *The American Journal of Occupational Therapy, 62*(5): 564–573.

Aubé, B., Follenfant, A., Goudeau, S. and Derguy, C. (2020) 'Public stigma of autism spectrum disorder at school: Implicit attitudes matter.' *Journal of Autism and Developmental Disorders.* https://doi.org/10.1007/s10803-020-04635-9.

Department for Education (2019) *Off-rolling: exploring the issue.* Available at www.gov.uk/government/publications/off-rolling-exploring-the-issue. (Accessed 17/03/2021)

Department for Education (2020) *Permanent and fixed-period exclusions in England.* Available at https://explore-education-statistics.service.gov.uk/find-statistics/permanent-and-fixed-period-exclusions-in-england. (Accessed 17/06/2021)

Department for Education (2021) *School workforce in England.* Available at https://explore-education-statistics.service.gov.uk/find-statistics/school-workforce-in-england. (Accessed 17/03/2021)

Domina, T., Penner, A. and Penner, E. (2017) 'Categorical inequality: Schools as sorting machines.' *Annual Review of Sociology, 43*(1): 311–330.

Goodall, C. (2018) '"I felt closed in and like I couldn't breathe": A qualitative study exploring the mainstream educational experiences of autistic young people.' *Autism and Developmental Language Impairments, 3*: 1–16.

Ljungblad, A.-L. (2019) 'Pedagogical Relational Teachership (PeRT) – a multi-relational perspective.' *International Journal of Inclusive Education*, https://doi.org/10.1080/13603116.2019.1581280.

Locke, J., Ishijima, E.H., Kasari, C. and London, N. (2010) 'Loneliness, friendship quality and the social networks of adolescents with high-functioning autism in an inclusive school setting.' *Journal of Research in Special Educational Needs, 10*(2): 74–81.

McShane, J. (2020) 'We know off-rolling happens. Why are we still doing nothing?' *Support for Learning, 35*: 259–275. https://doi.org/10.1111/1467-9604.12309.

Murray, D., Lesser, M. and Lawson, W. (2005) 'Attention, monotropism and the diagnostic criteria for autism.' *Autism, 9*: 139–156. https://doi.org/10.1177/1362361305051398.

Neca, P., Borges, M.L. and Campos Pinto, P. (2020) 'Teachers with disabilities: A literature review.' *International Journal of Inclusive Education*, June: 1–19. https://doi.org/10.1080/13603116.2020.1776779.

Office for National Statistics (2021) *Population Estimates.* Available at www.ons.gov.uk/peoplepopulationandcommunity/populationandmigration/populationestimates. (Accessed 19/07/2021)

Pearson, A. and Rose, K. (2021) 'A conceptual analysis of Autistic Masking: Understanding the narrative of stigma and the illusion of choice.' *Autism in Adulthood, 3*(1): 52–60. http://doi.org/10.1089/aut.2020.0043.

Wood, R. (2019) *Inclusive Education for Autistic Children: Helping Children and Young People to Learn and Flourish in the Classroom.* London and Philadelphia: Jessica Kingsley Publishers.

Wood, R. (2020) *Pilot Survey of Autistic School Staff Who Work or Have Worked in an Education Role in Schools in the UK: Initial Summary Report.* University of East London repository. Available at https://repository.uel.ac.uk/item/87w2v.

Wood, R. and Happé, F. (2021) 'What are the views and experiences of autistic teachers? Findings from an online survey in the UK.' *Disability & Society*, https://doi.org/10.1080/09687599.2021.1916888.

Wood, R., Moyse, R., Crane, L., Happé, F. and Morrison, A. (2021) *The Experiences and Needs of Autistic School Staff: Summary Report of Phase 2 Covid-19 Findings.* Autistic School Staff Project. University of East London repository: https://repository.uel.ac.uk/item/89318. (Accessed 28/08/2021)

PART 1

UNDERSTANDING AUTISTIC TEACHERS

Chapter 1

Special Interests and Their Role in Keeping the Teacher in the Classroom

Pete Wharmby

Before I start, please bear in mind this chapter is written primarily from my own experiences as an autistic, secondary school English teacher, combined with the experiences of other autistic education staff I have spoken with.

In many ways, teaching is not a very suitable career choice for autistic people. It is one of the more socially intensive jobs out there, demanding an awful lot of a person's extroverted tendencies and energy levels. Considering that the average autistic person is hyper-sensitive to sound and smell, the idea of spending one's time in a classroom packed with potentially boisterous teenagers seems rather terrifyingly misguided. The noise of a typical class of 14-year-olds can be overwhelming to even a non-autistic (neurotypical) individual, but the impact it can have on autistic teachers can be difficult to manage. Although admittedly not quite as bad as what primary school colleagues must experience, the shouting, laughing and various other sundry noises teenagers are capable of, and are enthusiastic in emitting, are anathema to many autistic people's sense of calm and safety. Add to this the giddying minefield of ever-changing deadlines, targets and assessments, as well as the stress of being around changing groups of large numbers of people for the majority of the working day, and it is frankly a wonder there are any autistic teachers in the workforce at all. There must be some kind of trade-off, some benefit that makes this discomfort worthwhile.

One almost universal trait of autism is what is known as the 'special interest' or 'hyperfixation', as I prefer to call it. When in the process of diagnosis, autistic people might be asked about topics, hobbies or interests that are particularly important to them, that are a refuge when feelings of stress are high, or all-consuming. As far as the autistic community is concerned, I believe that having hyperfixations is entirely normal and healthy, and many autistic people celebrate their interests and take pleasure in the fact they have these hobbies that mean so much to them, proud of the knowledge and understanding they have of these varied topics. These hyperfixations can be on any subject imaginable; the stereotype, of course, is trains and locomotives, with Pokémon and video games generally bringing up the rear. However, this is mostly a relic of the extremely male-centric world of autism research and discussion that dates back to the twentieth century, and is not very useful now, when we are increasingly aware of the huge diversity within the autistic community.

The reality is that if it exists, you can reasonably assume there will be an autistic person to whom that thing is the subject of intense obsession and time spent, from blankets to drain covers (both of these are special interests of people in my acquaintance) and pretty much anything in between. When engaging in a special interest, autistic people are typically calmer, more relaxed, happier and more focused than they would otherwise be – for many, it is a form of release or even self-medication: a well-timed foray into a special interest can stave off meltdown and be a generally extremely positive force in an autistic person's life.

But one thing is particularly important to my purposes here: our hyperfixations adore company, and if an autistic person is given the opportunity to share their passion for the subject with friends, relatives or complete strangers, then you can expect high levels of enthusiasm, enormous amounts of data and information to be delivered, and impressive levels of knowledge. In short, if you want to be taught something, you can do a lot worse than be taught about it by an autistic person for whom it is one of their special interests. I have been taught about various subjects by openly autistic people and the experience has invariably been truly fantastic, and my understanding of the topic afterwards deep and thorough. I remember learning a great deal about a strange video game called 'Five Nights at Freddie's' – a game where you must attempt to survive the titular work week in a fast-food restaurant haunted by deadly robots – from a 16-year-old student of mine; from just an hour talking, I knew more about that game than most. Autistic people can sometimes be genuinely very good at explaining and sharing their passions, either verbally or in writing. What if *this* is one of the reasons teaching is a counterintuitively excellent career choice for autistic people? Huge swathes of both the English Language and English Literature curricula are topics that I have a genuine hyperfixation upon, and I believe this has a vast pedagogical effect on the way I deliver the content and subsequently how my students perceive the subject, and even how they learn.

To be more precise about exactly how teaching a special interest affects my practice, I think it best to start at the beginning and explain how I feel when teaching content within the English curriculum that would not qualify as a special interest. I have always found teaching to be stressful and anxiety-inducing, and for much of my life and career assumed this was simply an inevitability – that teaching had that effect on everyone. Of course, I was mistaken in this, as there are plenty of teachers who do the basics of their job without a constant, gnawing sense of terror, and I wish these individuals all the best. For me, however, this was the reality. I would wake up feeling apprehensive about the day ahead, concerned whether I would be able to get through another five lessons of performing in front of 30 children. This fear would continue through the morning routine – a sense of doom (there's no other term that comes close), based on the simple reality that I didn't have the energy or wherewithal to work so relentlessly and exhaustingly for seven hours. And it would affect every instance of the morning, made even more stressful by having to complete the school run for my child too.

By the time I was sitting at my desk around half an hour before lessons began, the only way to settle my nerves was to log onto my computer, open up Wikipedia and read about the one thing that had the power to balance my anxiety and ease my mind: train wheel layout notation. This is a special interest of mine, you see: I find great calm and relaxation in studying the different shapes of locomotives based on their wheel layout (for example, how many driving wheels it has, if it has smaller leading or trailing wheels and so forth). After all, this is one of the main benefits of a hyperfixation; a source of calm to steady yourself through the stresses of life.

There was no way I would be able to teach the subtleties of a 2-6-2 tank engine layout to 12-year-olds, no matter how delighted they may be at the novelty. But it was different if I was teaching a special interest that day. English as a school subject for 14- to 18-year-olds is peppered with content that I could describe as a special interest. In English writing, I have my absolute and total devotion to good quality descriptive writing, clever simile and metaphor, and the use of techniques such as litotes (the use of understatement for comic effect) – all absolutely guaranteed to bring a huge bounce to my step if I realise these are featuring in today's lesson. In literature, I have my passion for ghost stories, dystopia fiction and comedy as genres (honestly, my very fondest memories of teaching are going rogue and introducing my 12-year-old students to *Three Men in a Boat* and the short stories of MR James). And in linguistics, my love of etymology, the history of English and its global reach... So much of the curriculum fits into the criteria of 'my personal hyperfixations' that the job, with all its stresses, strains, difficulties and impossibilities, became practically possible and even at times enjoyable as a result.

I certainly know when I am about to deliver a lesson on an aspect of English Literature that would count as a hyperfixation of mine. The anxiety I would normally feel about standing in front of 30 adolescents, chivvying them along to accept my understanding of the subject without protest, is wiped away, mysteriously absent. I am enthused, excited, genuinely pleased to have an opportunity to talk about this particular topic.

In these cases – reasonably frequent, perhaps once a week or so – I would leave the house excited, truly looking forward to whichever lesson it was; my usual feelings of anxiety and fear completely absent. It occurs to me now that this may well be how the majority of teachers usually feel, and it was such a potent difference to my normal state that if I had anything particularly stressful or out-of-routine to do, I would schedule a lesson or two focusing on a special interest to help me get through the day. For example, I might organise a one-off workshop on descriptive writing based on Gothic literature. It was on these days that I found genuine pleasure in the job.

I am known for being an engaging and passionate teacher amongst the students I teach, based on a combination of how I teach when I am genuinely enthused by a special interest, and how I try to match this when feeling otherwise overwhelmed, stressed and unhappy – a form of emotional masking. Over a period of several years, a teaching assistant I worked with regularly could tell when a lesson was delivered by the real enthusiastic me, or the masked, faux-enthusiastic version of myself. This was a revelation that I found troubling, because it made me question how attuned to this my students might be.

However, as with so many things to do with autism, it can be very easy to stumble onto negatives when wandering around and exploring the positives, and this subject is unfortunately no different. The first potential issue is to do with how autistic people generally present their special interests to others. The term 'info dump' is often used to describe the mechanics of this, the idea being that the autistic individual will, at length, reel off a long stream of information on the topic with little regard for the interest or enthusiasm of their audience. While this is an admittedly negative stereotype, many in the autistic community are happy to self-deprecate by recognising this as a part of their behaviour. However, talking at great length from the front is not a particularly useful pedagogical practice. In fact, it is possibly something many people will recognise as the antithesis of good teaching from their own school days, as it could cause considerable problems with students' engagement, retention and focus, ironically especially for neurodivergent students. There is a certain level of controversy around the idea of 'teacher talk from the front' pedagogy that I would rather not get into here, but I have certainly been guilty of verbally marching off for a good 40 or 50 minutes when I'm delivering particularly favourite content, such as the derivation of the English language and its historical journey, and I would gingerly suggest this may not have been the best way to deliver this information to the students.

There is also the problem of the chasm of experience and under-standing of a topic that special interests can create. At all times, the teacher is expected to have a higher level of knowledge and understanding than the student, but problems can arise when a teacher's knowledge is so far above that of the student that they find it difficult to pitch the instruction to the appropriate level. Some autistic people struggle to understand how their knowledge is not shared by others. For example, I have to work extremely hard to remember that my encyclopedic knowledge of the Marvel Cinematic Universe isn't necessarily shared by everyone I talk to, to the point where I can be genuinely shocked and dismayed if it transpires they don't know *xyz* about some minor, inconsequential plot point. It's long been my belief that it is this specific breakdown of empathy that could be the catalyst for the claims that autistic people lack 'theory of mind'. We have emotional empathy, but I feel sometimes we don't recognise that others lack the knowledge we have in our heads. If I do this when in casual conversation, then it stands to reason that I may do it when teaching a class about Dickens (most of his books class as a special interest for me, as does the Victorian setting).

A third concern, and this is something I will confess I have been guilty of, is that hyperfixation topics are so comparatively comforting to teach that non-special-interest content gets gradually squeezed from the curriculum – usually inadvertently – as too much time is sunk into working on them. I have had times where my mental health has been faltering and I have defaulted to hyperfixation subjects rather more often than I should, and find myself running out of time to deliver the rest of the unit. If I was having a particularly difficult week, struggling with work, home and my mental health, then I would often find myself dipping into the magic toy chest of my special interests too much, and finding my long-term planning suffering as a result. It's worth reminding here that teaching the same lesson or using the same resources is not necessarily a sign of laziness; more, it is a coping mechanism. In actual fact it's likely that lessons delivered while under the influence of hyperfixation on the topic will be intricate, detailed, hugely knowledgeable and delivered with great enthusiasm and joy. Laziness or an 'I can't be bothered' apathetic attitude don't really enter into it – it is far more about comfort and security, feeling confident in the material and desperately looking for some kind of solid ground to rest our feet on when the rest of the curriculum can feel nebulous and insecure. Many times when I was particularly struggling, I would find myself running to catch the class up to be prepared for their assessments. This had obvious drawbacks, not least in creating an artificially tense and fast-paced learning environment, which ironically are two things that any autistic student is likely to struggle with.

So there are ways that this magically energising phenomenon – one that may help autistic teachers overcome their anxiety and stress – can backfire and cause problems in the classroom. There is clearly a balance to be struck here: we want this level of passion and enthusiasm in the classroom from neurodivergent teachers, but we also don't really want said teachers to be struggling unnecessarily with an issue they don't feel comfortable discussing with their line managers. There was no point where I felt confident confessing what I have divulged here to my managers, for example.

There have to be ways of ensuring that this natural phenomenon is maintained whilst mitigating the less helpful effects. The first stage of this, as far as I am concerned, is transparency. Make absolutely sure that autistic teachers are comfortable to describe how their special interests or hyperfixations interact with their teaching practice in a non-judgmental environment, as early on as in initial teaching training if a diagnosis is known. If the profession is to be truly inclusive of neurodivergent individuals, then this is a necessary part of that, and needs to be weighed up against other known autistic traits that have an impact on teaching practice, such as sensory issues and organisational difficulties. At present, apart from in a few more enlightened oases of acceptance, school leaders and senior teams are ill-equipped to handle this level of disclosure from staff, as the base-level knowledge of how to adapt the job and working environment simply isn't there. Ensuring that teachers can discuss the impact of their special interests in the classroom without facing further scrutiny and loss of confidence is difficult; however this can be improved with sustained work. The ideal situation would be that an autistic teacher could go to their Head of department or their line manager – whoever is responsible for ensuring the curriculum is delivered in full – and explain how they are struggling with x element of the course, not because they lack the subject knowledge, but because they lack the enthusiasm and confidence to overcome the other barriers they face.

It seems to me vitally important that we manage to harness the hyperfixations of our autistic teaching staff across our schools. The benefits that autistic teachers provide are many and hugely varied, but the sheer passion and quality of understanding that autistic hyperfixation can bring is surely one of the most valuable things we can offer. In order to help facilitate this, I would like to propose here a series of steps that could be put into place to make absolutely sure this occurs. Of these five ideas, I suggest that step five is the most important, and as such have counterintuitively placed it at the end – you will see why when you reach it.

1. Ensure that it is known, at least by the Head of department (or equivalent) what these areas of extreme curricular strength are

One thing that never fails to make me feel valued is a line manager or colleague knowing where my strengths lie: in particular, my curricular strengths relating to teaching content. Being seen as the 'Victorianist' or a specialist in teaching writing skills makes me feel understood and appreciated. As an autistic adult, I am not hugely fond of being interrupted at lunchtime (too busy trying to decompress, ready for the next lesson), but if a colleague appears at my door seeking information about a special interest... Well, as an autistic adult, I can think of few greater opportunities and compliments! If an autistic staff member's areas of hyperfixation are known, it opens up avenues, such as allocating suitable schemes of work for either creation or adaption, or being the department guru on that topic. How 'out in the open' this would be in terms of disclosure of the diagnosis would be up to those involved, but it could easily go from relatively covert and subtle to absolutely open and obvious, whatever was to suit the individual.

A unit of work generated by an autistic teacher with a particular interest in that topic is likely to be a very useful resource for the whole department. I remember a unit I put together in my early years of teaching that was based entirely on one of my more niche interests – abandoned theme parks. I was at a school in Nottingham and the, then closed, American Adventure park was reasonably nearby; I created a scheme of work for different writing styles based entirely on this place, with newspaper report writing focused on the re-opening of the site, descriptive writing of the lonely, decaying rides at sundown and so forth. The students absolutely loved it.

2. Any hyperfixations that exist outside of the subject taught are excellent starting points for valuable extra-curricular activities

One thing that every school will always appreciate from a member of staff is the ability and capacity to run an after-school club, some kind of extra-curricular activity that adds life and variety to the usual menu that a school can offer to its students. Due to the stressful nature of teaching, as we have already examined, it is very likely that many autistic teachers would lack the energy or wherewithal to spend a further hour after school with the students, as by this time they may have been masking quite heavily for perhaps eight hours, performing the 'teacher routine' as their batteries rapidly drain. However, as with the main curriculum, if an autistic teacher has a hyperfixation that has the potential to act as the core of some extra-curricular club, then perhaps the school, students and teacher themselves can benefit from the teacher running a weekly session dedicated to their interest.

In my experience, this has frequently been a club for chess or other games, including the popular tabletop war game 'Warhammer', which has a keen autistic following. Personally, hyperfixation has led me to run several clubs dedicated to the paranormal – ghosts, flying saucers, that kind of phenomenon – and it is interesting how I had an absolutely unshakeable enthusiasm for such a club, with absolutely no real idea how to make it an actual interactive, worthwhile pursuit for the students! For the first few sessions we just sat around chatting about our favourite ghost stories until I realised we had to at least attempt something a little more tangible. As we looked at earlier, autistic hyperfixations can be very powerful in terms of generating personal enthusiasm and helping us push through energy barriers, but they are no guarantee of pedagogical quality. With enough support, though, encouraging autistic staff to flex their hyperfixation muscles a little can be a source of inspiration and brilliant outcomes for a school.

3. Hyperfixation with pedagogical subjects can be harnessed to help whole-school initiatives and provide good training and social media engagement

A team leader or line manager would be in a good position to notice if an autistic member of staff has developed a hyperfixation with pedagogy in general, or the social media networks that feed the recent uptick in teachers taking more ownership of their career development and training. The world of 'edutwitter', with its get-togethers, debates and relationships, can be quite intoxicating to anyone with an interest in social media and education. I well remember setting up my twitter account in 2009 (@commaficionado) as an education account, dedicated to live tweeting 'Teachmeets' and other events – this was long before I was diagnosed with autism. I had a hyperfixation with edutwitter for perhaps three years before I became rather disenchanted by the constant arguing. I had a blog, which later evolved into my autism blog, and I got into arguing about the importance of knowledge versus skill with some of the central players of the time. The key here though is how this was fed back into whole-school practice – as the school's resident tweeter, I became responsible for much of this new, collaborative practice reaching the rest of my colleagues, many of whom didn't even have a Twitter account. I hosted Teachmeets, shared good pedagogical practice and reviewed literature, none of it draining my batteries as it was a current special interest. It may not have been around forever – after all, some hyperfixations are temporary – but it had real impact while it lasted.

4. Allocation of autistic staff to subjects that lie outside of their comfort zones must be limited, if not avoided altogether

One of my most traumatic teaching memories occurred in my first year on the job. As a green, young Newly Qualified Teacher, I had a reasonably pleasant timetable focusing on different age groups to enjoy, and more free periods than I would ever have again. This meant I found myself having to cover other teachers' lessons fairly frequently. The first time I was placed in front of an unfamiliar class, I was in my element as the lesson was Geography and the topic coastal erosion: now this I could actually teach, as such things have long been part of a more all-encompassing special interest labelled 'physical geography but not forests' (for some reason the arboreal world has never fascinated me to the same extent as mountains, coasts and volcanoes). It was a class of 14-year-olds and my enthusiasm and confidence in the subject carried me along. In my naivety, I was pretty excited for my next cover lesson – what a great change of pace these were, what wonderful moments of variety. Unfortunately, my next cover was a Maths lesson. I do not wish to contribute to the strange British antipathy to mathematics as a discipline, but it is not my forte (though I'm perfectly capable at mental arithmetic) and, worse, I have no interest in it whatsoever. My special-interest-fed enthusiasm and confidence wouldn't come, and I experienced what it was to teach with zero hyperfixation support. I do not think I have experienced a longer hour than that lesson. Lack of confidence made classroom management seemingly impossible, and I had no reserves of extra energy to call up when required. In short, I was no teacher at all. It was then I was struck by how vital one's subject knowledge is in teaching, how linked it all is with the other, seemingly transferable skills of the job, such as organisation, behaviour management and so on. Or at least I feel this may be how it is for autistic teachers, who rely on the boost that their special interests bring them.

My second truly unpleasant out-of-subject experience was much later. I was Head of the English department and, looking back, at the top of my game. Autistic burnout was a year off and things were going reasonably well. However, I was given a weekly ICT (Information and Communication Technologies) class, as the computing department was down a member of staff, and save for video games, my enthusiasm for computing, spreadsheets, databases and such is fairly limited. Again I struggled, even with seven years' experience by this point, and I feel the experience was a contributing factor in my eventual burnout, which would come later in that academic year.

Forcing any teacher to teach outside of their specialism is a harsh necessity in modern schools, but causes lots of problems in terms of expertise and experience. With autistic teachers, though, I think it veers into the untenable – if our teaching practice is so underpinned by special interests that lacking it, even within our subject, can cause a drain of enthusiasm and capacity, then expecting an autistic teacher to teach totally outside of their interests *and* specialism is going to lead to negative outcomes.

I still have nightmares of teaching that class about Microsoft Excel, and they were actually a lively group of very pleasant, interesting students. Looking back, it seems strange that I would have had so much trouble with them, as I noted when teaching some of them English Language many years later. They shared the confusion, comparing those lessons with their experience of my teaching within English and coming to the conclusion I simply didn't 'get on with' Computing as a subject. I agreed with them. Such is the importance of our interests.

5. All of this must take place while simultaneously remembering the disability

The danger, after going through all of this, is that an autistic teacher is squeezed by their school of every drop of enthusiasm and energy their special interests may provide. Of course this would be a disastrous consequence and would contribute ultimately, as far as we know, to autistic burnout or worse. I have tried to communicate the idea that our hyperfixations can allow us to push past barriers that would otherwise halt us in our tracks; this has the potential to be a very powerfully good thing, but is also open to abuse. Teachers are prone to overworking themselves – autistic or not, the job is never really done. There is always more you could do. More that you *should* do. Spend an hour on teacher Twitter and you will find amazing work done by teachers who probably didn't really have the time to do it, and are in time debt with some other important part of their lives. Care should be taken when encouraging autistic staff to utilise the motivation and energy provided by special interests, to avoid contributing to burnout.

As such, it is vital that the disability is remembered whenever an autistic teacher is being encouraged to use their interests. An autistic teacher showing a surprising level of energy while doing task A, which is related to a special interest, cannot suddenly be assumed capable of task B, which is not related to a special interest. This is something I hear about frequently – an autistic teacher experiencing success and then finding all of their support structures removed or called into question, as if that one instance negates their need for reasonable adjustments.

There are ways to try to make full use of a teacher's special interests, and a key proviso is to ensure that people don't get taken advantage of, or bite off more than they can possibly chew. The importance of special interests in the classroom is, I think, rather underestimated and I feel that schools everywhere would benefit from a more honest conversation about what it is that enables autistic teachers to overcome any problems they may have and become extremely effective teachers. Sadly, doing this involves ensuring that everyone involved in the running of a school, from governors down, needs to be far more knowledgeable about how autism works and how it presents, so that expectations can be grounded, realistic and fair on all concerned. But with efforts such as this collaborative book, it seems we may be starting to make some genuine headway, and perhaps this generation of teachers will be the first to be able to utilise their special interests to the full, without fear of falling into one of the many traps I have outlined here. All students, neurotypical and neurodivergent, deserve to get the very best education, and autistic teachers have an enormously important role in this.

Chapter 2

Dealing with Change

Alan Morrison

Introduction

School life is one huge, never-ceasing whirlwind of change. Changes come in many shapes and sizes. Some are foreseeable and avoidable, others can be quite pleasant, and some come and smack you on the back of the head, creating dizziness and the need for a bit of a rest. However, I am sure that change may be dealt with, embraced and enjoyed – honest!

Much of what is written herein is based on my own understanding, tempered with input from learning about the experiences of other autistic staff. Thus, to restate what the reader may have previously heard regarding having learnt something of one autistic person, one has learnt something about just that autistic person. However, I think there may be some overlap with what I write here and there with the experiences of some other autistic (and even non-autistic) school staff.

Whether change derives from internal machinations of the mind or from the externally imposed world, it is needed in order to keep one truly interested in life. Otherwise, one may suffer from cognitive inertia and terminal thought vegetation, which, although sometimes feeling nice and secure, can be a trap.

Changes in school

Some of the types of change that can cause autistic staff extra difficulties are those that cause a shift in one's expectations or understanding of things. For example, nearing the start of a recent academic year, I believed that one of my classes would be hosted in a particular room only. Later I discovered this mutually agreed plan had been retrospectively changed without consultation with me, leaving me totally shocked and bemused: why was I now asked to teach this class in different rooms throughout the week?

Changes that are repeated in short succession again and again can cause a rather dizzying and overly anxious feeling. This is particularly the case when combined with other stressors, such as the social aspects of pupil interactions. For example, I recall classes I've had that sometimes got me stressed to a point where my usual classroom social scripts were simply insufficient to account for relatively small, yet frequent, changes in my understanding of what social narratives were unfolding throughout the lesson. This, with the associated heavy cognitive demands of keeping pace with such an ever-changing mental landscape, meant that anxiety would build on anxiety, spiralling towards shutdown.

Changes that push you towards meltdown-/shutdown-type events can pounce on you out of the blue. For example, if I encounter someone who is feeling upset, this can cause my emotional state to be very perturbed. Once, I was in a meeting when someone entered partway through, in what was (I retrospectively realised) a very disturbed state of mind. Being unprepared for this, and not recognising the shocking and distorting effect this spectacle had on my emotional state, I rapidly headed for a wee (i.e., small) meltdown. What I should have done was head for the door, accompanied with some excuse, in order to get some recovery time.

That said, some changes can be invigorating. I recall two separate occasions, 15 years apart, when a pupil asked me if I found teaching to be boring as they thought it was a rather repetitive type of occupation. On both occasions my response was that every day was different and thus not boring. By far the most salient thing in a teacher's life is other people: pupils/students and colleagues. As pupils and colleagues are human beings, they are in a constant state of change, emotionally, socially, intellectually and in terms of health and well-being. Therefore, one is constantly dealing with change throughout the day. I think the point is not to expect change to be totally eliminated from working life, rather to manage oneself and one's environment (social and physical) as best as possible.

For example, as we have moved from a 'brand them, stamp them' educational model to a 'carrot and stick' and now a 'relationship-based' system, one must deal with the ever-changing mix of individual character traits, personalities, social structures and environmental conditions that exist on a day-to-day, and moment-to-moment, basis. These can influence the near infinite (at least it can feel like that) interactions, thoughts and decisions – not to mention emotional experiences – that we all have. This is exhausting. However, if one works with understanding colleagues, such constant change can be taken in one's stride, like a contented leaf flowing along Csikszentmihalyi's river (Stevens 2007) – cheesy I know, but I like it!

Communication

Interpersonal communication between autistic and non-autistic people can, at times, lead to misunderstandings. This tends to be onerous, with stress and reduced cognitive capabilities sometimes being the result for considerable periods of time. This adds to the burden of doing one's job well, which can itself be stressful as autistic folk do like to 'get things right'. Interpersonal interactions inevitably involve emotional state changes, for which staff (autistic and non-autistic alike) may have the extra task of managing both their own emotions and those of others too, and this can be an immense challenge due to occasional hyper-empathetic-esque feelings (to coin a phrase). In my own personal journey of autistic self-discovery, the revelation that some of the emotions I feel are not my own has begun to help me manage social interactions with less anxiety and stress. When one works with empathetic and kind colleagues, stress may be reduced or even eliminated altogether, thus allowing one to fire on all cylinders, be a more effective contributor, and happier too.

Conversations with colleagues come in many forms, be they formal or informal. I really like formal conversations, as the subject of what we're discussing makes it easier to understand the parameters that shape the meaning of the conversation. This manner of language use tends to be safe in that one is relatively unlikely to say something inappropriate. This pertains to both my colleagues and me. I really like informal chat too, as I get to express myself in a much more fluent and subtle way. This can be good for deepening human-to-human social bonds which can lead to supportive relationships. However, there is an increased risk of boundaries being breached. These may be social boundaries, perhaps due to miscommunications, or professional boundaries, if one gets carried away in the moment.

Personally, I find extra processing time necessary to keep myself safe and secure whenever there is a mix of formal and informal, which is where things can get a bit weird. For example, say in a formal meeting, colleagues start off at some informal tangent, I may not have noticed this and thus have no idea what they are talking about or exactly why they are talking about it. The significant issue is that there is a sudden unforeseen and undisclosed (at least to my autistic brain) change in conversation that can leave me wondering if I missed an email, have nodded off, or maybe my colleagues have been involved in some invasion-of-the-alien-life-form-body-snatchers plot. All with resulting anxiety, an instant drop in cognitive abilities and the dread of worrying about not being able to do one's job correctly, and so on to the vicious downwards cycle of miscommunication and misunderstanding.

Something I've found that helps me in these situations, and that I've grown to like, is taking minutes during meetings. When you are taking minutes, you are not expected to be so involved in the discussion – woo hoo! Also, when you are taking minutes, one may reasonably ask that the agenda is adhered to, which can help avoid unforeseen changes in the topic of conversation that can cause so much confusion. Sometimes I have found myself asking for clarification over who said what, but within a context that looks quite normal or socially acceptable (so to speak), and as I am taking the minutes there is also at my disposal, to some extent, a way of pacing the conversation. Having an agenda in advance of meetings is a really good thing. It can help avoid some unforeseen, potentially wobbly-brain-inducing moments, and also provide a bit of much-needed extra processing time that may otherwise be absent during the often too-rapid conversation once a meeting gets underway. Thus, one is able to contribute more effectively to the smoother operation of the school. Again, the theme of *how* people work together appears to be a significant factor in my algorithm-like coping strategies.

It is sometimes assumed that we all share a common understanding of reality. However, if there's one thing that learning about social life has taught me, it is that this is often a rather dodgy assumption. This is also true in schools. Here I define social life as any shared activity, for example using shared systems to report on pupils' performance or working on a shared project. Anxiety stemming from the insecurity of one's model of reality may be drastically increased, in an instant, due to even a small detail in one's plans being altered. This can cause cognitive function degradation which in turn can lead to miscommunication between colleagues and so on, leading to a vicious circle of miserable existence (sometimes for the non-autistic staff member too).

How colleagues can help

I find the definition of autism as 'a way of processing the world' to be helpful – the world of school offers a lot to process, so please be sensitive to our sensitivities so we may better process solutions to help the team. In order for us to continuously work well, not just appear to cope well, we need to be part of an inclusive work environment. One reasonable adjustment is for our colleagues to get to honestly know us for who we are. Thus, they may work with us, and us with them, without pushing us towards being overstressed – indeed, this sounds like a success strategy for all. At which point it is important to remember that autistic folk are very much like other folk, but nearly always much nearer that emotional/cognitive breaking point. Hence, please be kind. And in relating specifically to the concept of change, maybe we need to accept that 'there should be a balance between focusing on control/certainty and accepting uncertainty' (Vermeulen 2020, p.4) in our working life.

Something I wish my colleagues would do is give me more time. This can be done simply by taking time to slow down whenever talking with me. Not talking slooooowly as such, more just allowing a second or two before expecting a reply and making it clear that they are ok with me taking a moment extra. All too often schools are places where things are done at break-neck speed, where even a one second pause may feel like a long time.

Something beneficial that I have become aware of is when a colleague notices that I have had a downwards spiralling event, and realises that we both therefore need an extra moment to process what has happened. I can then do a mini-paradigm-shift to ensure the small, but significant, detail remains just that. Otherwise, a 'small change' may mutate into a source of self-doubt, loathing and an all-round festering sore point that poisons one's relationship(s). Some self-awareness, discipline and compassion may help here. Merely asking, for example, 'Are you ok?' or 'Would you like us to clarify that?' can be sufficient. Sometimes I have found it useful to be told to go away and think something over and to respond by a certain time. This bypasses my unfortunately learnt behaviour of trying to keep up with a conversation that goes too fast for me to accurately engage with, and thus helps to avoid mistakes.

There's lots to deal with in a busy school day which is, of course, a normal school day. And then, as sometimes happens, after weeks of getting used to the pattern of daily and weekly routines, a change may be imposed; perhaps due to pupils changing classes or a colleague changing their role within the school. For example, if I am asked to take on another class, I am quite perturbed, disturbed and a bit discombobulated too. I have had experience of this where my colleagues who were most directly involved with this change demonstrated their understanding of my fragile nature. They supported me by helping me to find the easiest route towards my new weekly timetable, resulting in my team-based robustness evolving. This was despite this easiest route for me being less than the best immediate outcome for them. It gives me confidence to know that such kind folk exist.

In summary, dealing with change as an autistic teacher can be really difficult. That is, of course, unless you work with colleagues who know you're autistic and take a moment to check you're ok. Having reasonable support from understanding colleagues can go a long way to helping us deal with this and making schools better places. Colleagues can make or break it for us. We are the team!

References

Stevens, R. (2007) 'Person Psychology: Psychoanalytic and Humanistic Perspectives.' In D. Miel, A. Phoenix and K. Thomas (eds) *Mapping Psychology*. 2nd ed. Milton Keynes: The Open University.

Vermeulen, P. (2020) 'Coping with uncertainty.' *Scottish Autism*, 25 August. Available at www.scottishautism.org/sites/default/files/coping_with_uncertainty.pdf. (Accessed 05/01/2021)

Chapter 3

Mentorship for Autistic School Staff

A PREREQUISITE FOR CAREER SUCCESS

Yasmeen Multani

Teaching is a career that many teachers relish, and it can be an incredibly rewarding profession. Trainee teachers embarking on a teaching career are provided with a mentor for personal support and this mentorship continues throughout a Newly Qualified Teacher's (NQT) induction year (National Education Union 2018) in the UK. Yet, beyond the induction year, it is unlikely that mentorship will continue, as teachers are viewed as experienced. For many teachers, mentorship is no longer required. However, for Autistic teachers, mentorship should continue beyond the induction year, as the challenges associated with autism are lifelong (The National Autistic Society [NAS] 2021a).

What is mentorship?

The Chartered Institute of Personnel and Development (CIPD) (2020) in the UK describes mentorship as a relationship where a more experienced colleague supports the development of a less experienced member of staff. This definition aligns with the mentor–mentee relationship that exists during an NQT's induction year. The CIPD (2020) further suggests that mentorship is comprised of two-way relationships that involve a partnership of sharing and learning, and is, therefore, potentially mutually beneficial. This means that partnerships with Autistic mentees are not just beneficial for the Autistic members of staff, but also for the mentors, as this process can deepen their understanding of autism.

Not all mentorship relationships are formal: some – like those I will describe in this chapter – are informal. Essentially though, they are still comprised of mutually beneficial two-way partnerships that involve sharing knowledge and learning from each other. It is important to note that mentorship, whether formal or informal, can be a highly effective way of retaining Autistic school staff, and it can also ensure they thrive and progress in their careers, just as their non-Autistic colleagues do.

Critically, with just 22 per cent of Autistic people in paid employment in the UK (NAS 2021b), we need to ensure that Autistic staff are recruited, engaged and retained in the school sector, and that there is a better understanding of the barriers they face and the benefits they bring. Mentorship is an effective reasonable adjustment under the remit of the UK Equality Act (2010) that can provide the opportunity for employers to offer personalised one-to-one support to Autistic staff based on their needs. Support in the form of mentorship is also a powerful well-being tool and vital for Autistic school staff, particularly as research shows that Autistic burnout is one of the primary reasons why Autistic school staff are no longer working in schools (Wood 2020). Considering this, it is therefore reasonable to suggest that mentorship could be a way of retaining very valuable employees, who have the potential to impact positively on the life of the school community. In this chapter, through a phenomenological account of my experiences in educational settings, I will demonstrate the effectiveness of mentor–mentee relationships.

The challenges in a school-based environment

Teaching was certainly a career where, initially, I thrived. I worked in the same school for more than ten years and progressed from a parent-helper role to middle leadership. I was always eager to go to work and teaching was an incredibly rewarding profession. However, this was only until I no longer had the support from a particular person: my informal mentor. In the absence of a mentor, my career eventually collapsed. This failing career began with a reduced capacity to function and being unable to meet important deadlines and ended with Autistic burnout and trauma that is still ever-present.

You see, I am an Autistic teacher and school was often an overwhelming place, where it was difficult to cope with change and the 'unwritten' rules were a continuous source of anxiety. The daily assault on my senses was intense and often resulted in meltdowns, mostly in private, but on occasions in the presence of colleagues, which inevitably led to me being known as 'highly sensitive'. My meltdowns resulted in self-esteem-damaging labels being applied to me, such as 'confrontational', 'blunt', and 'rude'. When you do not know you are Autistic, as I didn't at the time, these negative labels can have a detrimental effect upon self-identity and eventually damage one's self-confidence.

In the past, situations occurred in the school where conversations with uncomprehending colleagues could impact negatively on me. For example, when I said I could not tolerate sudden change, it was automatically assumed that this was a 'fixable' problem, with the remedy being for me to practise regularly getting out of my 'comfort zone'. I was expected to continuously embrace change by not reacting and having positive facial expressions and body language. Indeed, if I could be positive about sudden change then, surely, I would no longer be Autistic!

These kinds of expectations, which essentially aimed to provide me with strategies to make me like everyone else, can result in trauma. The impact of this trauma for me was fear and anxiety during interactions, making effective communication challenging. A communication disconnect then occurred, and when the social communication problems are situated solely with the Autistic person, this further exacerbates the communication disconnect. However, according to Milton (2012), it is both parties that experience a problem communicating, referred to as a 'double empathy problem'; a shared problem based heavily on reciprocity.

How my mentor helped

As I have explained, life as an undiagnosed Autistic teacher was always full of challenges, with change being the one that affected me the most.

For example, a colleague leaving was devastating and unscheduled changes to routine unbearable. However, I felt safe to discuss my anxiety around change with my mentor, who provided reassurance and an open door for when I needed to talk things through. Sensory modality difficulties also troubled me; I have vivid memories of not being able to process speech sufficiently to understand others when background noises were overwhelming. Fortunately, it was no trouble for my mentor to write important details down and give me the information that way, instead of relaying it verbally. Break-time bells were also a sensory nightmare, but even though the bell did not appear to impact others, my mentor ensured that the bell was adjusted so that I would feel comfortable. My well-being was important to my mentor, and I always felt that my mentor listened to understand me rather than simply to respond.

I believe my former mentor knew me well, always adopting a person-centred approach and accepting my differences. This person was fair and consistent, and I always knew what to expect. Meetings were mostly arranged by me and if a period without contact had occurred, then my mentor would check in on me. Support was always tailored towards my strengths and there was no attempt to 'fix' me. My Autistic identity was accepted and I certainly did not feel that I needed to mask my Autistic traits.

As a result, mentorship was not just key to ensuring I was able to function in the workplace (with a high level of well-being), but it also helped me to feel confident enough to progress in my career. Undoubtedly for me, it was with the continuous support from my mentor that I was able to progress from the role of parent-helper and begin the role of middle leadership.

Dealing with the lack of a mentor

It was not long after my induction year that I had the opportunity to apply for a middle leadership post. By this point, my mentor had moved on and, despite the pain of adjustment to new leadership, I managed to succeed at the interview and initially everything was going well. However, the school was experiencing a high turnover of staff, and while trying to cope with the absence of my mentor, I was also concerned that highly valued colleagues were leaving, and unfamiliar colleagues were arriving.

In two years, I was led by three different Head teachers. By this point, I self-identified as Autistic and openly shared this with colleagues, but it felt like no one could understand me. I simply could not cope with all the changes and I felt as though I could not be myself any more. I had to mask my Autistic traits for almost two years to appear competent and, on most days, I went home exhausted and in tears. I was melting down daily and crying on my way to work. Eventually, this period of transitional change became overwhelming for me, and while trying to explain that I was finding things difficult to a senior colleague, I had a meltdown, resigned and went home.

It felt like my world had ended, but after some persuasion from colleagues I had worked with for some time, I returned to work. This was a mistake on my part: I only felt able to mask for a week, and at the end of that week, I had another meltdown in the presence of senior leaders. It became increasingly difficult for me to communicate effectively using speech, and I had little alternative but to take a long period of sickness absence. I knew at this point that I needed a period of recovery. I did not return to work after this; my written resignation had been accepted and I was in Autistic burnout. I consider that many of these difficulties may have been avoided if I had been provided with a mentor.

Since leaving the school where I worked for many years, I have been unable to stay in employment for more than nine months, despite now having a formal autism diagnosis. For years, I moved from school to school, desperately seeking a similar professional relationship like the one I had with my informal mentor, but I was unsuccessful. I was searching for what could be described as some of the essential qualities of a mentor: someone who is understanding, accepting of difference, straight-talking, a good listener, responsive and with a consistent approach to support. Furthermore, a mentor with the confidence to critique whenever necessary, but in a respectful manner. When led by a person with these noted qualities, I functioned well and was able to help and support others too.

I am still the teacher I always was, but I firmly believe that the one thing missing from the unsuccessful parts of my teaching career is that mentor-type person. In the new schools, I tried to build positive relationships with colleagues, but I did not feel safe expressing my difficulties, and there was no critical friend to support me. Having a mentor had enabled me to function well and the absence of a mentor resulted in Autistic burnout. This demonstrates that for me, an Autistic teacher, a mentor is crucial to well-being and success in the workplace.

Given that according to Wood (2020), Autistic burnout was a significant reason for Autistic staff no longer working in a school, it would be reasonable to suggest that Autistic members of staff should be offered a mentor as a form of support, not just so they can progress in their careers, but also to retain Autistic staff. From a neurodiversity perspective, offering mentorship to any member of staff who needs it, for as long as they need it, would be good practice.

Returning to the education profession

Seven years after the abrupt ending of my most successful teaching experience, I am now beginning to achieve career success once more. I am teaching again, not in a school, but at a university. In my new role, without even realising, a more senior colleague has become my mentor. I did not request a mentor and this person does not have a 'mentor' label, but quite naturally my colleague and I work well together. I am happy and excited about the future as I have found a mentor-type person who understands that I am different. I feel like my potential is recognised and that I am gently encouraged to do more, without me feeling overwhelmed. I feel confident to ask questions when I need clarity and I feel this clarity is provided without judgement. Sometimes, I need repetition of key points as I struggle to retain information that is communicated verbally, and it is refreshing to see information repeated as a matter of course. On occasions, my direct speech can be perceived as 'bluntness'; however, my mentor asks for clarification of meaning, instead of taking offence.

I strongly believe that if I moved to a different university and undertook a similar role, my level of well-being would not be as high as it is right now. It is never the job, for example, how easy or hard it is, how enjoyable or unenjoyable it is, but, rather, the positive relationship I have with a 'mentor'-type person that enables me to achieve success in my career. It is knowing that this person is available to listen to me and understand me that makes me feel safe and secure in my role. There will always be change, uncertainty and sensory stimuli that can overwhelm an Autistic person in a work building. However, for me, an Autistic teacher, the presence of a mentor is both calming and reassuring. I know there is someone there who can help me when I am feeling overwhelmed and my brain empties of all strategies for coping.

How to be an impactful mentor

In this chapter, I have argued that a mentor does not always have to be 'official'. It can be, for example, a colleague with whom the Autistic person has developed a positive relationship. It can be someone who is understanding and skilled at expressing empathy, so Autistic staff do not feel overwhelmed in their job, and most importantly so they know they are listened to and understood. Martin, Barnham and Krupa (2019, p.71) propose that mentoring should involve 'active listening': it is the empathetic disposition of the mentor that is also highly significant and their ability to listen carefully to understand the neurodivergent person. The CIPD (2020) also emphasises the importance of listening in a mentoring partnership. When an Autistic member of staff discloses that they have experienced an Autistic melt-down, it is appropriate to offer to reschedule a meeting if the Autistic person wishes to do so. This flexibility on the part of a mentor can reduce overload for the Autistic member of staff and thus possibly avoid further meltdowns. Asking an Autistic colleague about their communication preferences also provides choice regarding modes of communication and shows respect, which can help an Autistic member of staff to feel valued.

It is the kind of mentor skills mentioned throughout this phenomenological account that I believe could help to retain Autistic staff and gently encourage them to progress in their careers. A non-Autistic person, without lived experience of being Autistic, may never completely understand their Autistic colleague. Crucially though, it has always been beneficial to my self-identity when another person seeks to understand me, as it helps me to feel validated and supported. It is far easier for an Autistic person to share what is causing distress with a colleague who understands. A person who does not minimise a problem because they are not experiencing it, such as the loudness of a particular sound. Instead, a person who demonstrates understanding by acknowledging that a certain sound could be painful for their Autistic colleague, and then working collaboratively to find a reasonable solution. A person who understands that although they may enjoy spontaneity and surprise events, sudden change and uncertainty could overwhelm their Autistic colleague to the point of Autistic meltdown. This understanding can develop over time when the mentor becomes better acquainted with the Autistic individual. Indeed, just as mentorship is a two-way relationship (CIPD 2020), so too is communication, where both Autistic and non-Autistic people need to endeavour to understand each other (Milton 2012).

I, an Autistic teacher, am privileged to have worked with two colleagues who are both highly effective mentors. As the needs of Autistic staff based in educational settings are not always understood or adequately addressed (Wood and Happé 2021), it would be reasonable to suggest that mentorship training may be necessary to meet an Autistic colleague's needs. It is also important to note that this mentorship training should be designed and delivered by Autistic people (Milton *et al.* 2017; Martin *et al.* 2019).

Mentorship can be an effective reasonable adjustment that enables the school to find out what the Autistic member of staff needs to function well on an ongoing basis. This is more likely to be successful if the mentor adopts a person-centred approach to ensure that one specific approach is not adopted for every Autistic person as there is diversity in all people. Mentorship is not just a way of ensuring equality under the remit of the Equality Act (2010); it can also help to retain Autistic members of staff while facilitating career progression. Mentorship can provide opportunities for Autistic members of staff to achieve career success, just like their non-Autistic colleagues do.

References

Chartered Institute of Personnel and Development (2020) *Coaching and mentoring: Identify ways to apply coaching and mentoring principles as part of an overall learning and development strategy.* Available at www.cipd.co.uk/knowledge/fundamentals/people/development/coaching-mentoring-factsheet#gref. (Accessed 23/04/2021)

Equality Act (2010) United Kingdom. Available at www.legislation.gov.uk/ukpga/2010/15/contents. (Accessed 14/06/2021)

Martin, N., Barnham, C. and Krupa, J. (2019) 'Identifying and addressing barriers to employment of autistic adults.' *Journal of Inclusive Practice in Further and Higher Education, 10*(1): 56–77.

Milton, D.E.M. (2012) 'On the ontological status of autism: The "double empathy problem".' *Disability & Society, 27*(6): 883–887.

Milton, D.E.M., Sims, T., Dawkins, G., Martin, N. and Mills, R. (2017) 'The development and evaluation of a mentor training programme for those working with autistic adults.' *Good Autism Practice, 18*(1): 25–33.

National Autistic Society (2021a) *What is autism?* Available at: www.autism.org.uk/advice-and-guidance/what-is-autism. (Accessed 18/02/2021)

National Autistic Society (2021b) *New shocking data highlight the autism employment gap.* Available at: www.autism.org.uk/what-we-do/news/new-data-on-the-autism-employment-gap. (Accessed 19/02/2021)

National Education Union (2018) *The role of a mentor.* Available at: https://neu.org.uk/advice/role-mentor. (Accessed 18/02/2021)

Wood, R. (2020) *Pilot Survey of Autistic School Staff Who Work or Have Worked in an Education Role in Schools in the UK: Initial Summary Report.* University of East London repository. Available at https://repository.uel.ac.uk/item/87w2v.

Wood., R. and Happé, F. (2021) 'What are the views and experiences of autistic teachers? Findings from an online survey in the UK.' *Disability & Society.* https://doi.org/10.1080/09687599.2021.1916888.

Chapter 4

Inclusion Isn't Just for Children

THE MARGINALISATION OF AUTISTIC EDUCATORS DUE TO ABLEISM IN SCHOOLS

Kieran Rose

The role of the teaching assistant has always been a complicated one. Over the last 20 years, it has developed from 'parent-helper' to front-line specialist supporting children who experience barriers to academic education. Through my twenties, I spent ten years as a teaching assistant (TA) in two schools at opposite ends of England. I started out as a volunteer and quickly moved through qualifications to become a Higher-Level Teaching Assistant. During that time, as an Autistic person, I experienced a gamut of issues that, when I look back now, cause me to wonder how I managed to navigate them.

When you think about the role of the TA, it is one that comes with an enormous level of responsibility, but very little professional recognition or financial reward. The 'parent-helper' lens is often the one TAs are seen through, no matter how many qualifications they gather, or how professionally they do their job. Added to that is the fact that the specific challenges and barriers that come with being a TA are infrequently recognised. These can be exacerbated tenfold when that TA is Autistic.

Supporting children

Being an Autistic person surviving in a world where being non-Autistic is centred in every walk of life is difficult enough, but the specifics of working in a school environment can make that so much more complicated, particularly for TAs. As a TA, you are expected to work closely, usually on a one-to-one basis or with small groups, with the children who find academic learning the hardest. Often these children are known collectively as children with SEND (Special Educational Needs and Disabilities), a name that clumps together children with a whole range of differences, including physical disabilities and learning disabilities. Some children have what are termed 'behavioural' challenges, although in my experience that is more about their needs not being correctly met, rather than them being the cause of the problem.

A TA is often left to work with these children with minimal support and training on their specific needs, with no flexibility or autonomy and the highest of expectations of 'results'. TAs often take it upon themselves to research the needs of the children they are working with in their own time and at their own expense, because they are left with little option to do otherwise. But it's because of this and the time they spend closely working with those children, that it's not unusual for the TA to develop strong bonds and relationships with them.

In my role, I was teaching, validating, offering emotional support and friendship, being a confidant, often the person the child turned to at times of need during the school day. But despite all this, in my experience, it is usually the TA's knowledge regarding that child that is the least utilised and, after the child's, their voice that is heard the least. I think it's partly because of that lens we are looked at through: the parent-helper, rather than the professional.

The frustration this generates is immense. As an Autistic person, being 'not heard' is an everyday occurrence for so many different reasons. So common in fact, you'd think we'd get used to it, but we never do. It hurts, particularly when it applies to your intense and deep knowledge about a subject, often stemming from 'monotropism', a tendency to have very deep and strong interests (Murray, Lesser and Lawson 2005).

Contrary to popular belief, I think that Autistic people can be like sponges when faced with other people's emotional states. When you empathise deeply and connect with a child, see them struggling and know intrinsically why this is happening, not being listened to can be very painful.

For example, being asked to teach Autistic children to 'make conversation' was very upsetting for me, as was the requirement to expect eye contact and turn-taking from them. Similarly, teaching them not to talk about their interests, because they were considered boring for others, was an expectation I struggled with. The invalidation of the child's natural communication was deeply frustrating, as well as, of course, being highly problematic for the child.

Eventually, I decided to employ the same techniques I had learned from my work in a Forest School that seemed much more effective. Everything I did was framed around validating the children in every way possible. In my then-limited fashion (because I was not diagnosed at the time), I was helping them understand that, because it wasn't natural for them to act in the ways other people did, they might find the world difficult. They needed to understand that there was nothing wrong with how they did things, but until they were older and had more control over their lives, the expectation was always going to be that they went about things in the ways they were told.

Autistic masking

I'd never heard the term 'Autistic masking' by this point in my life. It was something that was only being discussed by Autistic people on obscure parts of the developing internet. Nevertheless, a part of me, even without that language and those concepts, understood intrinsically that those children were engaging in, and being encouraged to engage in, masking. It came with the realisation that masking was something I also actively participated in, because my life was about making other people feel less uncomfortable around me.

Nowadays, I write extensively about Autistic masking (Pearson and Rose 2021). In relation to my current work, it's what I 'cognitively fell in love with'. Masking can be defined as a trauma response (Rose

2018), a psychological safety mechanism made up of complex layers of physical, emotional and social actions which an Autistic person is driven to use to self-protect and project an acceptable version of who they are. This can occur by applying – in fluctuating degrees – often decontextualised and sometimes rehearsed learned behaviours to certain situations. At the same time, the Autistic person suppresses natural behaviours, self-identity and reactions to the sensory environment. This can look like being the 'quiet one' or the 'people pleaser'. Conversely, it can also mean projecting an exaggerated identity, such as the class clown, or the 'naughty child', feeding the confirmation bias of those who are around you: giving them what they want and expect to see.

All of this happens partly consciously, with the person quickly learning in childhood to dissociate from the act, and from then on unconsciously: pre-emptive, reactive and unplanned. And all at great mental and physical cost. In terms of my experiences, looking back I see my projected mask as a person who fawned and kept quiet. I projected that I would do anything for anyone, even to the detriment of myself.

Dealing with change

One of the biggest challenges in my work as a TA came around routine and consistency. Autistic people and the need for routine are common bedfellows in the Autism narrative. What I know now is that need for routine is born out of the uncertainty we constantly have regarding the world around us and the anxiety that stems from that. Every moment of our lives is spent second-guessing our actions and being confused about the actions of non-Autistic people, which is solely pinned on us and is interpreted as us having deficits (Milton, Heasman and Sheppard 2018).

So, because of that, consistency and routine become really important to Autistic people. They are things you can rely on; they aren't going to cause surprises.

But…

There is very little consistency in the working pattern of a TA. Each day is usually different to the last, different from hour to hour even, with constant last-minute changes and last-minute instructions on who to work with and how. The last-minute task could be an admin duty, such as an enormous pile of photocopying, but without being given a timescale to do it. I was never actually given any time to do the photocopying, as I was expected to be in class. If there was a lack of communication and joined-up thinking, I would be left floundering.

For an Autistic person, each of those last-minute things was like a tiny death, actually painful, physically and mentally. We're back to monotropism again, because attention is not only about being in cognitive love; attention can be focused on anything. It's whatever you are doing in a particular moment that engages you. When you are monotropic you lock onto that thing. Your senses are engaged with that thing. You must build up energy to get into it and once you are there you enter what is called a 'flow state', where everything in your body is flowing towards the task in hand (McDonnell and Milton 2014). So, any deviation, any pull away from that flow, is difficult to deal with.

I needed forward-planning, clear and direct communication, consistency, more autonomy and trust that I knew what I was doing. But most importantly I needed to be validated and seen for who I was: to be seen through a lens of strengths.

Love for the job

My biggest strength was that I loved being a teaching assistant. I was good at it. I loved being with the children, seeing the spark in their eyes when the pieces fell into place and the things that had previously tormented them suddenly made sense.

I loved being with the Autistic children most of all; always arguing that the best way they learned was to find things that excited them, because that was when they threw themselves into a subject and wanted to know and understand *everything* about it. It never occurred to me that the reason this filled me with so much joy was because this was exactly how I learned. Back then, I was advocating for monotropism before I even knew what monotropism was.

Spending time with those children, building those relationships, was pure joy. It was always done on a non-hierarchical level too. While the boundaries were always there for me, I like to think that I was a safe person to them, that I was able to develop a more horizontal relationship with them than the teachers. Safety and trust are so integral to Autistic children. Especially, I realise now, when that safety and trust is a reflection of relatable experience, of shared communication styles and an awareness of connection unavailable between non-Autistics and Autistics. Community connectedness is vital to the emotional well-being of any Autistic person (Botha, Dibb and Frost 2020).

I strongly feel this is something that all schools could benefit from. Staff whose experiences mirror those of the children they are supporting. What better role-modelling is there than sharing relatable experiences that have positive outcomes?

Disclosure of diagnosis

But this is where the most difficult aspect comes in. To be that role model, you need to disclose that you are Autistic.

In my first school, immediately after my diagnosis, I'd disclosed it to the Head teacher and told several colleagues whom I considered friends. I quickly discovered that disclosure and being 'out' were not the same thing. I naively assumed that to tell my employer and colleagues would automatically mean I would be accepted, that I could be open about who I was and that if any problems arose, the fact that I was Autistic would be considered. I believed that it was a foundation for working together to help me be better at my job.

Unfortunately, my first disclosure in a work setting was met with disbelief and it took me a long time to get over this. This made me wary of disclosing my diagnosis in subsequent work settings. I was genuinely scared as to how I would be treated. What good would it do me? I simply didn't have the language to challenge colleagues' pre-conceived ideas about autism. I then had a difficult experience when I felt forced to 'out' myself in a group situation. This marked the beginning of the end of my time as a TA.

I had spent a lifetime masking, projecting a version of me that other people found vaguely acceptable. But in that time of post-disclosure, this projection slowly, like at other points in my life when things became too much, started unravelling.

Sensory issues

I now became consciously and acutely aware of the impact of the sensory environment around me. Little things like the sensation of school glue on my fingers that made me feel sick to my stomach, the smell of the kitchens and the dining hall, which were unavoidable if we had an indoor PE session.

I hadn't realised how much the sensory environment within the building had been overwhelming me. I'd find moments where the light shining, mottled, through the dirty windows was catching on dust motes dancing like a choreographed ballet and I'd be hypnotised, literally switched off to everything to the point where the children would have to nudge me to 'wake me up'. Sounds became louder and more painful, lights were brighter and more painful, smells stronger and more overwhelming.

Larger things consciously impacted me too, such as skin-to-skin touch, which had always caused me enormous pain, akin to the sensation of having a molten hot branding iron pressed against my skin, but which now progressed to a pain response when people came too close or brushed up against me. These things are unavoidable when working in close proximity with children.

All this, I realise now, had been impacting on me all along. But I'd dissociated from most of it, shoving it deep down inside me; but now I was awake to it which somehow made it all the worse.

Burnout

My confusion increased and I was constantly losing words, barely able to string a sentence together. My periods of verbal Autistic shutdown were increasing; the situational mutism which had plagued me all through my life was back with a vengeance, words repeatedly stuck painfully in my throat. The world felt like it was spinning out of control as I became more and more burnt out.

The energy that had previously been poured into the bottomless and constantly demanding mask was suddenly gone, and I was left bereft and gasping for air. None of it made sense and I was exhausted from trying to make it make sense. I'd spent years trying to do and be what everybody else wanted me to do and be, and now I couldn't do it anymore. Honestly, it was like watching a car crash in slow motion, as I became more and more aware that I was unable to maintain this other version of myself that had existed for so long.

With hindsight, I know I was experiencing Autistic burnout (Raymaker 2020), a common theme discussed amongst the Autistic community, but insufficiently recognised in the professional world. It's the result of spending all your energy trying to exist in a way that others find acceptable, but which isn't authentic for you. It's often finally triggered by something traumatic.

Life on every level became more and more difficult after this, impacting on my relationships outside of school, particularly with my partner; and there was a further, more worrying impact on my mental health. So I did the only thing I could without losing everything: I walked away from my job.

Autism training

In my experience, most Autism training in schools reinforces tick-list-style thinking, where the individuality is forgotten when Autism is mentioned and the same supports and supposed 'reasonable adjustments' are consistently wheeled out, for every child, regardless of their individual needs. That training also often reinforces conformity, the putting in place of behavioural thinking and methods of control that are a faux version of actual support for children, essentially framed around making the school's life easier, because that child becomes more manageable.

Reflecting back on my time as a TA, the children I supported were experiencing exactly the same stigma, ableism and requirements of neuro-normalcy that I and so many others experienced as undiagnosed children in schools decades earlier.

And sadly, those same things still happen to a large extent today. There is still a huge lack of understanding in schools of what

Autism really is and what it means to be Autistic. It's still grounded in deficit and, unfortunately, as schools come under more and more pressure for academic achievement, it's often those with the most need of differentiation and individualised learning who are least likely to be provided with this.

Glimmers of hope

There are glimmers of hope though.

What is really significant is that a decade ago, the book you are now reading wouldn't have existed. It is encouraging to see a shift towards more books on Autistic learners; for example, Rebecca Wood's wonderful book (2019), and other books and research that factor in Autistic perspectives and experiences in schools. That educators are reading these, and hopefully taking on what is offered within them, leads me to hope that Autistic children and Autistic staff are going to be validated and supported more and more.

I think knowledge and understanding around Autism in the wider world has increased, which has put pressure on schools to make changes, but that is also wrapped up in the emergent wider societal revolution in how we understand identity and the many different things that incorporate identity. Moving forward in this way can only have a greater benefit not only for Autistic children in schools, but also Autistic adults.

There needs to be so much more recognition that as adults we experience the same levels of invalidation as the children in our care; that we have to sit with the same expectations; that we are making the same adjustments as the children; and that we're doing all that with the extra levels of responsibilities of adulthood.

As Autistic people, our knowledge and experience about ourselves holds enormous value, not only in respect of helping future generations of Autistic children to understand and advocate for themselves, but in supporting children and adults from all backgrounds to further understand the importance of the diversity that exists all around us, particularly when it comes to neurotypes.

We do that by harnessing that knowledge. The application of

that knowledge can not only help shape educational practice, but also help everyone in education – children and adults – develop a broader understanding of the world.

I now work as an openly Autistic person who trains and consults to organisations all over the world. This includes one of the settings where I had worked as a TA, but this time I am a respected professional, considered to have important insights to share. It is validating for me to know that I have transitioned from an Autistic person whose identity was a problem, to one whose knowledge and insight hold value.

There are school staff who can act as positive role models, who are exemplifiers to all, of the need for difference. They can help create safe spaces where Autistic learners can be authentic and validated in their Autistic social skills, communication and learning style; where they can learn from their non-Autistic peers and their non-Autistic peers can learn from them. Where those Autistic teachers and teaching assistants can utilise their monotropic brains and use all that knowledge for the most wonderful of learning opportunities. To be able to achieve this, Autistic school staff must also feel it is safe to disclose their diagnosis.

As a teaching assistant, all I ever wanted was to be able to do my job to the best of my ability, in an environment that met my needs and supported the needs of those who are like me. I felt my role as both a teaching assistant and as an Autistic person was vital to the education and well-being of the children I worked with, yet that wasn't always reflected in how I was treated.

I really believe that things can and will change, and are changing, but we do have a very long way to go.

References

Botha, M., Dibb, B., and Frost, D.M. (2020) '"Autism is me": An investigation of how autistic individuals make sense of autism and stigma.' *Disability & Society.* https://doi.org/10.1080/09687599.2020.1822782.

McDonnell, A. and Milton, D.E.M. (2014) 'Going with the Flow: Reconsidering "Repetitive Behaviour" through the Concept of "Flow States".' In G. Jones and E. Hurley (eds.) *Good Autism Practice: Autism, Happiness and Wellbeing* (pp.38–47). Birmingham: BILD.

Milton, D.E.M., Heasman, B. and Sheppard, E. (2018) 'Double Empathy.' In F. Volkmar (ed.) *Encyclopedia of Autism Spectrum Disorders*. New York: Springer. https://doi.org/10.1007/978-1-4614-6435-8_102273-2.

Murray, D., Lesser, M. and Lawson, W. (2005) 'Attention, monotropism and the diagnostic criteria for autism.' *Autism*, 9(2): 139–156. https://doi.org/10.1177/1362361305051398.

Pearson, A. and Rose, K. (2021) 'A conceptual analysis of Autistic Masking: Understanding the narrative of stigma and the illusion of choice.' *Autism in Adulthood*, 3(1): 52–60. http://doi.org/10.1089/aut.2020.0043.

Raymaker, D. (2020) '"Having all of your internal resources exhausted beyond measure and being left with no clean-up crew": Defining autistic burnout.' *Autism in Adulthood*, 2(2): 132–143. https://doi.org/10.1089/aut.2019.0079.

Rose, K. (2018) *The Autistic Advocate*. Available at: https://theautisticadvocate.com. (Accessed 17/06/2021)

Wood, R. (2019) *Inclusive Education for Autistic Children. Helping Children and Young People Learn and Flourish in the Classroom*. London and Philadelphia: Jessica Kingsley Publishers.

PART 2

INTERSECTIONALITIES

Chapter 5

Life on the Margins

A PERIPATETIC PERSPECTIVE

Madge Woollard

I work as a peripatetic piano and keyboard teacher, that is, a freelance teacher who travels between schools each week to deliver lessons. The dictionary definition of peripatetic is 'one who walks from place to place; an itinerant' (Merriam-Webster 2021). So, I am a visitor, an outsider, someone who is not integral to the day-to-day workings of a school. I identify as LGBT and non-binary, and I was diagnosed autistic in 2016. This means that I am marginalised on multiple levels.

I have been teaching in schools since 1997, after completing a music degree at Cambridge University and a Post Graduate Certificate in Education (PGCE, a teaching qualification) as a junior school teacher with a music specialism. My original intention was to teach classes, but I had to abandon that dream after repeatedly failing at interviews. I applied for over 60 jobs and was called for at least ten interviews, but was never offered a post. I was the only person in my PGCE year who left college without a job lined up.

In hindsight, the reasons why I was passed over were most likely linked to my autism. I was not very confident or articulate at the time, and I have always been somewhat unconventional in my appearance. But it has worked out for the best. Classroom teaching would probably have been too much for me, and I work far better in a one-to-one setting. In addition to private teaching, I currently work in three schools: a large secondary school (for pupils aged 11–18), a mainstream primary school and a small religious primary school (for pupils aged 4–11).

My story

Music has always been my passion. There are often strong links between autism and music. Music is built up of logical patterns, and when combined with our enhanced auditory sense, it can invoke intuitive responses in some of us. My early sensory responses were clearly connected to the workings of my autistic brain. The first chair I learned to clamber onto, aged two, was our piano chair, and I was fascinated by my mum playing nursery rhymes to me. I went for lessons aged five. I used to dance around the school playground every Wednesday, knowing that after school I would go to my piano teacher's house. She would talk to me about dinosaurs and anything else I was currently interested in, as well as showing me the fascinating workings of the black and white keys.

I loved going to church at this time too and would sway in time to the singing of the Lord's Prayer. After a couple of piano lessons, I picked up how music was notated, and wrote out the opening of the tune of my favourite hymn, 'O Come, O Come, Emmanuel!', by ear, impressing the adults around me. Shortly after this, we relocated to London and I had no lessons for a year, until my junior school music teacher was able to take me on after school.

My big musical break came aged 11 when I passed the audition to the Pimlico School Music Course. Pimlico was a huge central London state secondary school with a difference: a handful of students each year were selected for the scheme, which meant free top-class tuition on two instruments, musicianship classes, choir, orchestra and ensembles. I loved school in general: the work, the routine, the structure and most of the teachers. In fact, without the music course, I'm not sure how I would have survived my teens.

I was always on the margins. By my second year, I had begun to realise that I was markedly different from my peers socially and could not relate to most of them. I experienced what would probably now be called 'selective mutism', often going whole days at school without speaking to anyone other than to answer the briefest of questions. I spent break-times in the music practice block, alone with a piano. It was far preferable to the noisy din of the playground, where I had no friends and was constantly verbally bullied. Music was a safe haven for me. It engages the whole of me: it is aural, visual and kinaesthetic.

At school, it left little room in my head for reflecting on my social failures. Moving my fingers across the piano keys and listening to the beautiful sound of the chords and harmonies was immensely comforting, like a stim for me.

With my parents' help, I applied for an organ scholarship at Cambridge University. My school Head of Music told me it would not be worth applying, because I would not get it. I proved him wrong. In September 1989, I became the first ever female organ scholar at Peterhouse, Cambridge's smallest and oldest college. I enjoyed it there, but socially it was again a disaster. I always assumed that once at university, I would find 'my people'. I thought that as organ scholar, and leader of the chapel choir, I would be at the centre of college musical life, but yet again I found myself on the margins. I realised early on that the drinking and partying lifestyle of many students made me distinctly uncomfortable, and I just wanted to get on with my studies. I did not realise at the time that I was LGBT, although I had a vague idea that I might be bisexual. I had no relationships while at school or university, although I really wanted to. People generally gave me a wide berth. As I watched most of my acquaintances coupling up, I began to wonder whether there could be something innately wrong with me. I blocked out this thought as much as I could, with more music and more studies.

Teacher training

After completing my degree, I enrolled on a PGCE course for primary school class teaching, specialising in music. I experienced discrimination during my teaching practice. I worked very hard, read every book on the recommended reading list, spent all hours in libraries looking up resources and prepared perfect lesson plans. In class, I thought I delivered the lessons reasonably well, and built up a rapport with some of the students. However, I was told by my supervisor that I was 'not doing it right', and that although the content of my lessons was fine, my 'delivery' was not. I was never told what I should do differently, just that if I did not improve, I was going to fail. Yet again, I was being marginalised.

I know now that I communicate in an autistic style: I am sincere and passionate; I care deeply about each of my students, and my manner is gentle. But I can also be very direct and sometimes monotonic, and my eye contact is unusual. It was not uncommon, back in the 1990s, that no one picked this up, and the fault was assumed to be within me. I passed the course, but never received feedback about what I had done 'wrong'. I desperately wanted to improve, but genuinely didn't know how. I now know that it was the supervisor who was failing me, rather than the other way around!

Starting out

I wrote to many schools in my local area asking if they needed a music teacher but got next to no response. I then began my peripatetic teaching career by joining an agency of music teachers. This helped me initially to find work, but the agency had a number of problems, eventually going bankrupt. Since I began to teach privately, most of the work I do has come from word-of-mouth recommendations by other teachers or students. It is often hard for autistic people to get a foot in the door, as we don't make contacts or connections easily. It is important for people to see us doing our jobs and doing them well, and often unexpected links are then made. I believe I have been very lucky in that respect.

Difficulties in schools

I often feel uncomfortable in school, because I feel very different to the other staff and because the environment can cause me sensory difficulties. I am still very much on the margins.

For example, communicating with diverse individuals (juniors, teens, students with a vast range of abilities and from different cultures) is draining. I don't talk as much to students as some teachers do. Talking can tire me easily. I sometimes stumble over my words and my intonation. While I can talk quite easily about the theoretical and practical aspects of music, talking about emotions is difficult at the best of times. I tend to become very awkward when emotions are expressed, and don't always know how to respond. I like students to explore for themselves, and for the music to speak for itself. This approach does not suit every student, and I am aware that for some of them, my teaching style does not match their learning style.

Although I go to school primarily to do a job, and have built up some good working relationships, I would still like to feel a little more included socially. Many of the staff ignore me in the staffroom, and I do not have any contact with them outside school. I only know the names of three or four teachers at a school, even if I've worked there for years. I used to be invited for end-of-term meals, but the invites stopped. I always felt like a fish out of water on these excursions, but would love to know why I am no longer invited. I think I am generally viewed as odd: I live with my wife; we are childless, vegan and don't drive. I see these as positives, but I sense that some colleagues find it hard to relate to these things that are so far outside their experience.

While I do not currently require any accommodations for my autism, I do experience some challenges. Sensory issues have become worse in my forties. Schools are frequently noisy, smelly places, full of sensory bombardment. I often spend hours in a windowless room with fluorescent lighting, which gives me a headache. Or I am asked to move rooms at short notice, sometimes mid-lesson, because another teacher needs the space. In one school, I have to lug the keyboard across the noisy playground to teach in the dining hall, where staff are still clearing up after dinner. The smells of dinner, coupled with the clattering of crockery and background chat of the dinner staff, can make me feel quite ill. On other days, my teaching space is at the top of a stairwell, meaning I have to carry the keyboard up, and lessons are sometimes interrupted by staff and pupils walking through. Previously I have worked in the 'baking room', where staff would regularly interrupt me to turn on ovens, microwaves and even the washing machine. I try to minimise sensory discomfort by focusing on the job and the student. I often spend my evenings in almost total silence in order to recover.

Positive experiences

Overall, I love my job, and there are many positives. I think I have a lot to offer my schools. I am a competent musician, and good at what

I do. I think it is great for the kids to see someone who is noticeably different, sharing their passion and offering an outsider's perspective. I have built up strong connections over the years with several of my neurodivergent students; I feel that we understand each other well.

As a self-employed teacher, I have a lot of autonomy and control. My job provides structure and routine in my life, which is very important to me. Having regular lessons with each student at the same time each week is comforting for me. I am good at time management, which suits my job well. I am sharing my special interest and getting paid for it, which is a dream for many, and I enjoy the energy and enthusiasm of many of the kids. I benefit from certain aspects of contact with people and contributing to the bigger picture of their overall education. I enjoy pushing my boundaries and moving outside my comfort zone, despite the challenges this presents.

I believe that meeting my wife Jo in 2000 had a hugely positive impact on my teaching. I am happy and well supported in my home life, and I feel able to be authentically LGBT. While I generally don't discuss this with students as it is not relevant, I do not hide it either. Jo is also autistic. She works as a counsellor and is much more empathic than I am! Knowing that I can talk through any work difficulties I have with her, and that she will view them from an autistic perspective too, is immensely important to me.

In conclusion

I think we all have work to do to be more inclusive, to meet each other halfway. It should not just be the work of autistic people to educate everyone else. In general, I'd like to see school staff making more of an effort to include all those on the margins of their workforce. This goes for other employees who are not present for the whole school day, such as cleaners, midday staff and caretakers, who I have often seen treated as second-class citizens within the school hierarchy.

On reflection, my job as a peripatetic music teacher has suited me well and helped me greatly. It has been important in forming my sense of self. I am very proud of all that I have achieved in my career so far. In many ways, I am a lot less marginalised now than I was in my teens and early twenties. But I still have a way to go. I would like to feel I can be more open about my autism, so that I can bring my whole self to work and not have to hide a part of who I am. I would like to specialise in teaching neurodivergent students, with whom I generally get on very well, as we can be on a similar wavelength. I guess I will always feel like an outsider, but I am fine with that. I am proud to be different and proud to be who I am.

Reference

Merriam-Webster (2021) *Definition of Peripatetic.* Available at www.merriamwebster.com/dictionary/peripatetic?pronunciation&lang=en_us&dir=p&file=peripatetics_1 (Accessed 22/03/2021)

Chapter 6

What Does Autism Look Like?

EXPERIENCES OF A MIXED-RACE AUTISTIC WOMAN

Jade Ponnudurai

The interconnected nature of gender, race and disability has informed my entire five-year experience of working in schools and colleges. It has impacted all of the various roles 1 have undertaken, which include learning support, teaching and middle management. 1 now work as an Autism Hub Coordinator for a local authority, but in this chapter, 1 will reflect on my experiences in schools and offer suggestions for how my current work provides a model that can benefit autistic pupils.

While still undiagnosed, 1 began working in schools as a teaching assistant and quickly fell in love with the role. 1 enjoyed both the pace of the classroom environment and supporting children and young people in their learning and pastoral care. Having diagnoses of dyslexia, dyspraxia, PTSD (Post-Traumatic Stress Disorder), anxiety and depression, Ehlers-Danlos Syndrome and with an autism diagnosis pending, my passion for disability studies grew.

This was massively encouraged by my positive experience of working in that same school with a small group of boys with learning difficulties, all from ethnic minority backgrounds. They needed support in their English studies, and 1 taught them basic animation techniques to inspire them. This meant they could animate the characters in the book they were studying and thus approach their learning goals from a different perspective. This classroom experience gave them the opportunity to learn in a safe and nurturing environment, whereas before they had struggled with expressing themselves and being heard. I made it creative and fun so that they could see that learning could be enjoyable.

At the end of this series of special sessions, we staged an exhibition in the school so that they could demonstrate their work to their parents, carers and fellow students. The Deputy Head attended to give a welcome speech and praised the boys for their new skills and their work. I was very happy to be able to frame their attainments in this way and for them to experience public recognition of their success in front of their peers, school staff and families. This was especially important to me as it was a school in an inner London borough with a high level of violent crime and anti-social behaviour. Young people, especially those from ethnic minorities, were perceived to be at risk of becoming associated with gangs and county lines.[1] It felt important to show these young boys that education could be fun and a pathway to a better future.

As well as the insights I have been able to offer, I have always found that my own experiences of disability have helped me to connect well to the groups I was working with at any given time. Being autistic has made me better able to respond to the needs of children and young people from a perspective of deeper understanding and empathy. This was whether I was teaching aspects of multi-culturalism to a pre-entry class of non-speaking autistic students with profound learning difficulties, or teaching English to a group of vulnerable and looked-after students aged 16.

These experiences led to me to enrol for degree studies, first in Special and Inclusive Education and thereafter in Special Educational Needs and Disabilities (SEND). These qualifications resulted in me quickly being appointed to roles with additional responsibilities, such as learning support coordinator, team leader and safeguarding officer

---

1   County lines: when illegal drugs are transported from one area to another, often across police and local authority boundaries (although not exclusively), usually by children or vulnerable people who are coerced into it by gangs (National Crime Agency 2018).

within a specialist provision. I was also a trainee English teacher. However, the more responsibility I had within these roles, the more I felt I was experiencing the discrimination and challenges that came with them, through being a woman, being mixed-race and, especially, through being autistic.

I often wonder if sometimes people thought that I was being competitive in the workplace, when in fact I was just being autistic (as yet not officially diagnosed) and approaching situations from a neurodivergent perspective. I tend to be very logical in my approach and not afraid to challenge when I think something is incorrect. I can come across as forthright and blunt or without nuance. I adhere strictly to rules and work by the book. This has meant that colleagues didn't always understand me, and on occasions I have felt overlooked when I could have made a positive contribution. Additionally, my youth was an issue: I could be mistaken for a student and my experience was sometimes questioned.

I have a very strong sense of justice. Perhaps this is because I am autistic, but also because I have already experienced discrimination in my life. Being eligible to access disability support makes me even more aware of the inequality and inequity in support allocation for disabled people. It also makes me want to strive even harder to bring about change for the disabled community. When I was working in schools, if I noticed any discrepancies in the quality and level of support experienced by some young people with SEND, I was always hugely motivated and inspired to try and do better by them. I wanted to make a difference. I advocated on behalf of the students (and their families), and put a lot of time and effort into making sure they received the best support possible, so they could access their education, feel and be safe, and transition effectively into adulthood. I felt that this did not always chime well with some colleagues, who seemed to think I was too much 'on the side of' the students.

While I was working in schools, I would encounter some outdated attitudes towards autism and disability generally. Such attitudes, including the belief that autistic people could never get a job, could also have hindered the support for autistic pupils, and have a negative impact on the aspirations of the students themselves.

As is often the case with autistic women and girls, I only received my diagnosis of autism as an adult (Gould 2017). When I advised my workplace of my diagnosis, having already been working in my allotted role in middle management, I felt there was an overall lack of understanding of the link between mental health and disability. Management and Human Resources seemed to display a very different attitude towards me, and I had the distinct impression that, from their point of view, my diagnosis simply meant more work now that they had an increased duty of care towards me to make reasonable adjustments. I didn't feel that my needs were adequately assessed, and not all adjustments were provided. For example, I was supposed to get my own desk and space, and be allowed to work with headphones to help block out extraneous background noise, but sadly this did not happen. I worried that if a disabled member of staff was not adequately supported, then a pupil with special needs could not be supported either.

Happily, not everyone took this approach. One college reacted very well to my pending diagnosis and highly appreciated all the random amounts of accumulated knowledge I had on disability and funding for pupils with SEND. They referred every funding query to me for clarification and affectionately nick-named me 'the fount of all knowledge'.

As a woman of mixed-race and working with predominately white staff, I seemed to always be allocated the ethnic minority students, those with a difficult history, a criminal past, or anyone who had previously been a youth offender, in a gang, or who was deemed hard to handle. To me, it seemed as if being mixed-race somehow aligned me with these factors by virtue of the black side of my heritage. My perseverance in the workplace paid off, however. My intense and dedicated involvement with these young people meant that I was able to gain their respect and trust, and slowly their behaviours improved.

Once I received my autism diagnosis, random parts of my life seemed to fit together like a jigsaw and everything started to make a new and precious sense. I am happy and proud to be part of the autistic community, even though several negative life events happened around the time that I received my diagnosis which had the effect of tainting that experience overall. Therefore, my situation is very much a work in progress, and I am still trying to figure everything out. Even now, with my diagnosis confirmed, when people find out or are informed that I am autistic, they often do not want to believe me, saying things like 'but you look normal'. Some people appear reluctant to accept autism in adults, believing it to be something that autistic children have but will grow out of. It seems difficult for some to accept that I lead a daily life just like they do, that I can function in society and do not need a carer, for example.

Another issue is that unconscious bias, whether it applies to race, gender or disability, is prevalent in schools. It is also my experience that disability within ethnic minority communities is often approached with less overall understanding and more feelings of shame within the family and community, which can cause additional conflict. Autistic men are also always assumed to be white, which can make it difficult for men of other heritages to get a diagnosis (Obeid *et al.* 2021), as well as acceptance in the community. There is also a lack of support material available for autistic girls and women, making it difficult for us to inform ourselves both before and after receiving a diagnosis, if we are lucky enough to get one at all (Carpenter, Happé and Egerton 2019).

While working in schools and colleges, I quickly realised that the bar can be set very low for support roles for pupils, often with no prior experience required. This means that there is room for ignorance and prejudice to thrive, leading to bad practice and a lack of interest and empathy. This can also mean that advice and suggestions from people with lived experience are not recognised or valued. Nevertheless, I have often taken heart from having the pleasure of managing teams of staff whose work ethic and dedication to their pupils have been exemplary. The passion, drive and skill they displayed in working closely with the group of disabled pupils could be inspiring and motivating.

I now work as an Autism Hub Coordinator for a local authority. This role falls under the adult social care sector as opposed to education. Having had time to reflect on my past career, I would like to suggest changes that could help raise overall awareness and even out the system of support in educational settings. I believe that if the education sector were willing to consider introducing a framework for schools and colleges that is similar to the Core Capabilities Framework for Supporting Autistic People (Department of Health and Social Care 2019), which is a legal framework enshrined in law for the English social care system, this would have the benefit of greatly enhancing everyone's overall experience. It would also enable better outcomes, for example, in understanding autism, providing personalised support, paying attention to physical and mental health, and tackling issues concerning risk and safeguarding. The fact that the Core Capabilities Framework is actively promoted, such as by Commissioners through free training, provision of support workers and being embedded in practice, means that it is implemented efficiently and practitioners can be critiqued on it and held to account. On the other hand, in schools there is currently no requirement to follow and implement the guidance from the Autism Education Trust, for example.

I almost feel that by working outside the education sector in adult social care, I can provide more targeted support and assistance to autistic children and young people than I could before. For example, despite having an Education, Health and Care Plan (EHCP) with defined outcomes, autistic young people can leave school without skills and with their outcomes not realised. This is where the adult social care service, for example, the Autism Hub, has to step in, to bridge the gap and offer support for young people through help with independent living skills and the transition to adulthood via peer and support groups.

Although I am no longer working in schools and colleges, the education sector will always remain close to my heart. I do not exclude the possibility of returning to the school environment in the future, but I would hope to see a great deal of change and modernisation take place first, especially in terms of how disabled students and staff are perceived and treated. I would hope to see schools give greater thought and weighting to their aspirations for their disabled students and staff. I would hope to see more adherence to disability laws and codes of practice. It would be my wish for people to be open to new models, new ideas and new research, for example, around safeguarding or looked-after children. Above all, I would hope that disabled pupils and staff would be consulted about change, as they need better representation and to be heard.

My most positive take-away from my work in schools and colleges has been the wonderful array of interactions I have had with the students during my time in my various posts. I have been able to position myself as a safe and reliable person for the pupils within what can be a bewildering system for them in school. I have boosted their confidence while also supporting their learning. I also feel that as a mixed-race, autistic woman, I have been a role model for them. They can see that being a woman, being mixed-race and having a disability are not barriers to progressing through life and achieving goals.

References

Carpenter, B., Happé, F. and Egerton, J. (eds.) (2019) *Girls and Autism: Education, Family and Personal Perspectives.* London: Taylor & Francis/Routledge.

Department of Health and Social Care (2019) *Core Capabilities Framework for Supporting Autistic People.* Available at www.skillsforhealth.org.uk/images/services/cstf/Autism%20Capabilities%20Framework%20Oct%202019.pdf. (Accessed 15/06/2021)

Gould, J. (2017) 'Towards understanding the under-recognition of girls and women on the autism spectrum.' *Autism, 21*(6): 703–705. https://doi.org/10.1177/1362361317706174.

National Crime Agency (2018) *County Lines.* Available at www.nationalcrimeagency.gov.uk/what-we-do/crime-threats/drug-trafficking/county-lines. (Accessed 10/06/2021)

Obeid, R., Bisson, J. B., Cosenza, A. *et al.* (2021) 'Do implicit and explicit racial biases influence autism identification and stigma? An implicit association test study.' *Journal of Autism and Developmental Disorders, 51:* 106–128. https://doi.org/10.1007/s10803-020-04507-2.

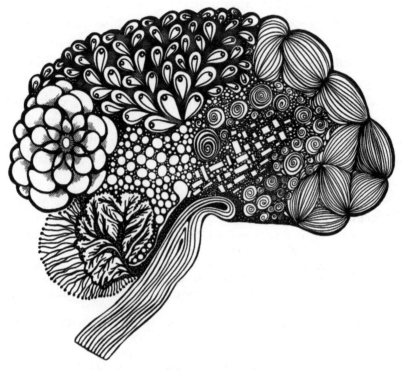

My Brain by Susanna Matthan

Chapter 7

Perspectives of a Well-Travelled Specialist Outreach Teacher in a Pupil Referral Unit

Susanna Matthan

In this chapter, I will explore how my different life experiences intersect with my understanding of what an autistic teacher can bring to the world of education. I was diagnosed as autistic and dyslexic in later life at the age of 52, having studied, lived, worked and parented without understanding why life seemed inexplicably difficult for me.

Educational background

I was born in Shropshire to a Finnish mother and a South Indian Malayali father. As a woman of mixed heritage who was educated in India, Finland and England, I have had privileged access to a variety of educational and life experiences.

Aged two-and-a-half, I attended a Montessori kindergarten in Chennai, India. Then I went to a mixed school for children aged 4–11, before moving on to a large girls school in Bengaluru. I spent the longest time in the girls' school and felt comfortable as it was a safe, leafy, expansive and mostly female space. There were no threats to me as a person and I did feel that, even though I was different, there were other girls who were also different in their own way. There were students from every part of India, of different religions and cultural heritages. My family then moved to Finland and I attended a *Lukio* (a school for pupils aged 16–18). Soon after that, I moved to England and went to an all-girls Sixth Form, then a Further Education College, and finally Art College. Subsequently, I went on to attend university and qualified as a teacher.

In every setting, where people are involved and systems are in place, there are rules of engagement, and the values become clear after spending time with the people who have helped create the environment. I observed and assimilated some new values from my educational experiences – from the strict, uniformed, formal, academically-focused Indian schooling to my laid-back, informal, casually-dressed Finnish education. The values were embedded in each space, forming the ethos, and setting expectations that I was not consciously aware of at the time. It is only looking back reflectively that has enabled me to realise how little I was involved in creating those spaces and how much they have affected me. It has made me think about how disempowered many children feel, even after attending a school for years.

My subsequent teaching career – in a mainstream school, a special school for boys and two Pupil Referral Units (PRUs, for children excluded or at risk of exclusion from school) – has drawn on my mixed heritage, my varied educational background, and the different social and cultural perspectives and values I have experienced and absorbed. These elements have enabled me to build a strong relational foundation and specialist expertise in my chosen field and were developed further during my work in the PRUs.

My work in Pupil Referral Units

My role assumed a range of skills, professional knowledge and competence, and I was expected to hit the road running. PRUs have several functions, from centre-based academic or specific focus group provision, to outreach in schools in small groups and one-to-one sessions. Staff were expected to work with all the children in the PRU and also to be outreach teachers. This required travelling to different schools on public transport and working with individual children who were referred to the service. I had to do all my own paperwork, keep up to date with any statutory requirements, manage my own diary and logistics, and claim my expenses. I had a full diary as I attended planning meetings, met with the referred children, designed bespoke support (which was reviewed regularly), and attended multi-agency meetings. As an outreach teacher, each member of the team was the face of the service, and so expected to offer advice, make decisions and have discussions with professionals, Head teachers, Special Educational Needs Co-ordinators, other outside agencies, parents and carers.

In some ways, I was able to adapt quickly as I thrived on pushing through when learning things that I was interested in. I also had the support of experienced colleagues within the team, but I was completely new to this way of working and had to dig deep and find alternative ways of relating. There was no hand to hold, no guide, just a map of the city. I just had a bus pass and the instruction to go and see these children. I was learning extremely hard things all at the same time, and sometimes we had supply teachers who came in for a morning, then left suddenly and never came back. Had I not had a supportive and empathetic Head of the PRU, I might have left or collapsed much sooner.

The work was difficult, especially as it relied on numerous interpersonal and intrapersonal interactions with a large number of people, demands and situations. Trying to meet the requirements of people under pressure made me even more determined to keep moving forward, because I do not give up easily. I knew there must be better ways of working, so I set myself tasks that meant I could focus on practical adaptations, drawing on my problem-solving skills in my own time.

The children I helped

I had entered a complicated world of excluded, often troubled, traumatised, or disaffected children and young people aged 11–18. Many of the children I met were despondent, seemed depressed, often reactive, or aggressive. Some of them were harming themselves; sometimes they were suicidal. The majority were boys, mainly black boys from poorer areas of the city, who had been referred for a range of issues such as physical attacks, sexual assaults or verbal abuse. Many of those referred had common factors that could not be ignored. They were unable to fit into the mould; they wanted to live without the constraints of a box; they spoke too directly and wanted autonomy. Very few children had any acknowledged disabilities that were recognised by the schools and the expectation was that the children had to adapt, adjust and do better. Essentially, the remit was for students to learn to behave nicely, or face exclusion.

However, it became apparent to me over time that the children who were perceived as a 'problem', or 'challenging', were really struggling to access an education because their needs were not met. Nobody had asked any questions about their individual needs and the perception was that some schools just wanted to move them on. For a select number of children, schools were prepared to let them attend the PRU for time-limited programmes, such as anger management courses. It was invariably about 'fixing' the child, though, and the threat of exclusion was always present.

On reflection, it is highly likely that many of these young people had undiagnosed conditions. I consider that many of them should have been appropriately assessed and might have had an autism diagnosis if the right people and systems had been in place. I could see the patterns, write reports, meet with relevant adults; yet there was always a steady stream of disaffected young people flowing through. These were children struggling to articulate their own needs, who were not being heard and were reacting to the restrictions that were around them. The young people themselves had no means of accessing an education that was suitable to their needs, despite the requirement that this should be irrespective of 'age, ability and aptitude and to any (Special Educational Need) he or she may have' (Department for Education and Department of Health 2015, p.216).

Over time, I noticed that excluded children were increasingly marginalised, isolated and pressurised to fit into an education system that did not acknowledge their lived experience, social reality, individual pace of growth and development. Young people were saying, 'This place is really damaging me, I hate my life, why are you doing this to me?' They were trying to communicate, but not in ways that complied with school policies, rules and regulations.

My approach

My first priority was to listen to and engage with each child. They often came with fat files of recorded misdemeanours, but I was determined to seek other sources of evidence. I could not rely solely on the reports provided by schools, so I began learning directly from the students I was meeting. I chose to focus on each child and on the reason for referral. I would meet anyone else in the life of the child that I could. I accepted every referral with equal weight and without prejudice. These children were used to being judged – often harshly – and punished for rule-breaking, but it genuinely didn't matter to me what the child had done.

I now recognise that being autistic has definitely influenced the ways in which I work, organise myself, and relate to people and circumstances. I had originally qualified as a Mathematics teacher, led there because I naturally perceive life in terms of patterns, shapes, order, detail and sequences. In my case, it is not about predicting, it's about whether things fit together. I'm reasonably good at spotting the *odd* things in patterns. My perception is that human interactions are based on patterns, despite being affected by constant change, activity, growth and progress. During my own autism assessment, the revelation that I was actually decoding every interaction came as quite a shock to me. Having spent so much time considering detail, patterns stood out as soon as I became involved in working with a new case, such as noticing that a child had been excluded every Friday for a term, or regularly truanted Physical Education or French lessons. I could use these observations and knowledge to ask questions and find out what was really going on in a particular setting.

The pressing need for a dynamic, relational model became the focus of my work, simply because I noticed that the children with the greatest unmet needs were the ones who were screaming silently and remained voiceless. I needed to be able to communicate with them in a way that suited their individuality. This was not an easy task, as many children had already shut down emotionally due to their experiences and did not want yet another adult telling them what they should be doing. Some were verbal and articulate, others barely spoke and needed other ways of communicating: it was my responsibility to find a way or refer them to relevant areas of support.

I started to pay deep attention, to listen to everything, give opportunities to change answers, focus on interests outside of school, to ask about family, loved ones, pets, significant events, hobbies. I showed up with colouring pencils, fidget toys, paper, play dough, plasticine, sketchbooks, and even tiny Lego® people. I frequently gave away sketchbooks if a child had no resources at home. As someone who does not fit a standard mould myself, I sought understanding of myself through creative expression and contemplation, increasing my ability to understand the needs of the young people and how to support them. I drew on the varied spiritual traditions of my heritage to spend time in silence and solitude.

The influence of my own educational background

I increasingly appreciate the culturally varied educational experiences that have shaped and moulded me, enabling me to use my neurodivergent interests in ways that I could never have envisaged in my childhood. For my own education, I had very little choice about where I went to school as my parents were responsible for these big decisions. I adapted and made the best of where I was placed, as I do now, seeking solace in my own internal world. Both my Indian and Finnish roots share a 'can do' mentality. The Finnish word *sisu*, loosely translated as 'perseverance, grit and guts', is part of my core. Professionally and personally, giving up on even one child was not an option for me. I can converse in different languages, adapt to life in different countries, connect with people – anywhere – so in my work, I always believed there must be something I could contribute.

Looking back, I am now aware that I was only able to pay the deepest attention to the things that interested me. Taught stories, text and literature became impossible for me to interpret within group settings as I rarely had the right answer. I still avoid reading fiction. This personal struggle has enabled me to reflect on the possibility that the children I was working with might also be struggling to interpret text, read social situations or access the curriculum from their unique perspectives.

I have also questioned the role of personhood in educational provision. I observed that many of the young people I worked with had some hidden creative interest, but they were rarely able to pursue it in school. I could relate this to my own academically competitive Indian schooling, which did not have a proper place for my creative expression. There was a sense that non-academic interests were for spare time, outside of school, and that school was for academic study and high achievement alone. However, I believe that each child is whole, has value and worth, and has gifts and talents often unrelated to academic performance.

Most of my own schooling, particularly in India, was based on academic achievement, and compliance, and was adult-led. In my earlier PRU days, I wondered why children were not able to just do what was asked of them, by following the rules and policies to secure their own future or academic achievement. I was slow to recognise that my own struggling academic achievement, and that of the children I was working with, may well have had underlying factors that were simply not visible or explored at the time. My own sense of self was slow to develop and I had limited understanding of how to advocate better for children.

My memories of attending school in Finland, however, were relaxed and calm, without pressure to perform and I have no recollection of ever being assessed. Perhaps I hoped that adopting a similar approach in my work in PRUs would enable children to want to be themselves. I focused on what was useful to each young person: drawing, talking, creating and planning. I also employed 'visioneering', a process of developing a mental picture of what could and should be happening in a child's life (Stanley 1999).

Successes and struggles

My primary focus was to maintain good professional relationships wherever possible, and I felt able to do this well because I was observant, patient and genuinely cared. I was present and held unconditional positive regard for the individual during our meetings. I was reminded of times in my own education (an art teacher comes to mind) where the adult was present, non-judgemental, accepting, often silent and allowed me to be creative.

My casework paperwork was of a high standard, all hand-written and passed on where necessary. I made sure that the things that were important to the young person were recorded, mentioned, highlighted and followed up with those who were responsible within each setting. Personal reliability, accuracy, attention to detail and hard work are values that were embedded throughout my own education and my wider family background, and I took care to maintain this in all aspects of my work.

However, there was a lot of pressure (probably from myself as much as external factors) to 'turn a child around' and/or 'fix' them, often in a short amount of time. I found this to be an entirely unrealistic, impossible task and often quite distressing. I was unable to 'fix' any child. It was an ongoing battle against those schools who did not want to spend too much time on a child perceived as 'needy' because they felt this was giving them undeserved attention or taking something away from the other children. The long-term emotional impact of this was exhausting.

When working one-to-one with children, a lot of the work was based on the school's reason for referral and what the referrer reported about each child. However, just talking about what the school had written about the child rarely helped. If anything, it made some children angrier and there were times when a young person refused to come to sessions because they felt that my role was the same as that of any other teacher in the school. Sometimes the relationship just broke down and sessions ended.

It really felt like a personal failure when a child I worked with was permanently excluded or moved elsewhere because they were not 'turned around' fast enough. The decision to exclude a child was made by Head teachers, never by me, but the sense of failure was always a tough professional blow. Children have very little autonomy in large settings, even less if their needs are not established. Too often children appeared to be dispensable and there was little understanding of neurodivergence, disability or an individual's changing developmental needs. If I had understood my own neurodivergence at the time, I may have been more persistent, fought even harder and demanded better provision for each child.

Positives and negatives

The most rewarding aspects of my work were, without doubt, the relationships I built with the young people. As a neurodivergent woman, I understood the importance of listening to each child; I accepted them and offered them a safe, secure space to be open about their experiences in schools.

Another significant transformative aspect of my work was being part of a team of professionals who supported each other with regular peer supervision and staff meetings, and who could be called on if needed. I had the support of my peers and felt respected, even when I made mistakes. It is through having such a positive relational model that I was able to grow personally and professionally as a neurodivergent woman. The knowledge and recognition that I mattered professionally also positively affected my work with young people.

Nevertheless, the weight of a full diary in an emotionally demanding role resulted in exhaustion. I didn't drive when I had my first PRU post, and covered many miles on foot and on public transport. It was emotionally and physically draining. I worked part-time, and it felt like I spent my days off recovering. Looking back, I realise I had missed the early signs of chronic fatigue and eventually I burnt out. My emotional and mental health were both at a very low point.

I also had intermittent periods of extreme professional self-doubt. There were frequent managerial changes to the ways in which we had to operate, new demands made of us as teachers, which I (and others) always took time to adapt to. We moved offices several times, often at very short notice. This was very difficult to live with.

The tendency of some professionals to blame the child or their parents was a prevalent narrative, and the expectation was that they should just try harder. Every single exclusion or placement that broke down had an impact on me, despite colleagues' reassurances that there was nothing more that we could have done. The feeling of not being good enough kept reappearing. The ever-present internal battle was distressing and took its toll.

The value of autistic teachers in PRUs

No child really wants to be made to feel different, excluded, removed from a setting or isolated in a booth when they are distressed, dysregulated or struggling. Adults who are present, safe, respectful, observant and aware of the small changes in a child's daily routine can make a world of difference. As attuned autistic professionals, we have so much more knowledge available to us that can enable children to be themselves in educational settings. When adults make decisions for and on behalf of children without their explicit voice, we risk failing them. The child's voice, whether spoken or communicated in an alternative way, is essential and has authority.

As autistic educators, we can bring our own reflective, empathetic insight into our professional life (McLaren 2013), enabling children who don't fit into the standard mould to thrive. For this to happen, autistic people of all ages must be included, valued, accepted and heard. I embrace my cultural heritage, my lived experience and my neurotype, and in reflecting on my own life experiences, I hope that I have served marginalised young people well.

References

Department for Education and Department of Health (2015). *SEND code of practice: 0 to 25 years.* London: DfE. Available at www.gov.uk/government/publications/send-code-of-practice-0-to-25. (Accessed 17 June 2021)

McLaren, K. (2013) *The Art of Empathy: A Complete Guide to Life's Most Essential Skill.* Louisville, CO: Sounds True, Inc.

Stanley, A. (1999) *Visioneering.* Colorado Springs, CO: Multnomah Publishers.

Chapter 8

The Intersection of Autism, Race and Teacher Training

Eiman Munro

Why did you decide to train to be a teacher?

It was in 2002, when a colleague cut out an advert for teaching from a newspaper. She placed it directly on my keyboard, in front of me. I was in my fourth year of a graduate placement and had just handed in my three-month notice to leave. My time as a trainee actuarial consultant was coming to an end.

At this time, I was not diagnosed with Autism, so I didn't understand why I found the open office environment to be problematic. At one point I thought my eyes were going funny. By that I mean I often had trouble reading documents from my in-tray. I remember getting so worried that I booked an eye test in my lunch hour, but nothing was wrong with my eyesight. I realise now that the difficulties I was experiencing were due to sensory issues caused by the busyness of the open office environment.

Another issue was that I had never been promoted like all the other graduates and I had trouble developing myself professionally as my anxieties grew with each year I was there. This became particularly difficult in the aftermath of 11 September 2001, when Islamic extremists hijacked four planes in the US, and flew two of them into the Twin Towers of the World Trade Center in New York. As a Muslim, I had become more paranoid as life changed for the worse during my underground train commutes to work. People would stare at me, more so than usual, and one woman even got off the train as I got on. I remember having a meeting once in a shopping centre and a young boy spat at me from above. I had to move the meeting to a new, more enclosed location.

On top of that, I found many times that colleagues would explain specific aspects of the work to me and I couldn't hear them. I thought I was lazy and undisciplined when it came to focusing on the job. As a result, I struggled to meet the financial targets each year to justify the company's investment in me.

However, supporting and training new graduates was an activity I found myself enjoying, as I gave them a few lessons or one-to-one support. This was my first experience in a professional capacity where I thrived. I could relate to the students and enjoyed learning to teach them. So, the cut-out advert from my colleague was perfect timing and gave me a direction to move into a career I hoped I might thrive in.

What influenced your choice of teacher training course?

After leaving my first ever full-time job, I was in a surreal juncture in my life, and an unpredictable one. For most of my academic life, things had been pretty much planned: school qualifications, university degree, job. Each stage was decided for me by either my parents or cultural expectations. For most Iraqis like me, there are two main career options, medicine or science, and indeed I had chosen to do my degree in Physics. Finding myself in a position where I did not have the next thing planned was exciting, and I knew only that I wanted to become a teacher.

I used that freedom year like a gap year. I did voluntary work with a local charity, where I learned about fundraising and how to support children from ethnic minority backgrounds. It gave me practice working with children and planning their activities, just like I would need to as a future teacher.

I then decided that, since I was making my own decisions, I would choose a course that was right for me. By now I knew how I studied best: this was self-study, in my own time. A flexible trainee teacher qualification (a Post Graduate Certificate in Education) seemed to tick many boxes, because I had two years within which to complete it and I only had to attend lectures once every two months. My chosen university was a little further than what I was used to in terms of commuting, but as I only needed to attend for one Saturday every two months, it was more like a day out than a rush to get to university. The off-peak time meant no crowds on the underground train, and so it became a pleasant journey.

What aspects of the teacher training course worked well for you and why was this?

First, it was a course that gave students two years to complete it. This allowed me plenty of time to manage my anxieties when it came to deadlines for essays and completing the school placements.

Another positive factor was that I chose to do my placements first and then complete the essays afterwards. This flexibility allowed me to set my own deadlines. This is because my mind works in a way I call 'modes'. I must be in a certain 'mode' in order to work to my best. So, when I am in teaching mode, I can't be in essay writing mode. The switching between the two functions could sometimes take days to achieve and maybe even a week, depending how tiring the school placement was. Hence why my essays were completed after all three of my school placements had finished. Also, completing essays after doing the practical work was useful for feeding into the writing.

Finally, even though I had two years to complete the course, I actually finished it within 12 months. The flexibility of the course worked so well that I was able to complete it quicker than I had thought.

Were there any aspects of the teacher training course that were less successful? Why was this?

Although we had lectures sporadically throughout the academic year, I found them difficult to get through. From a sensory point of view, lectures can be overwhelming. And, in my case, my mind tends to shut down when I am in a lecture theatre with lots of students. I remember there being lots of 'distractions' or sensory information to process. I am very conscious of my surroundings and must get to locations fairly early in order to take it all in and settle my mind. It helps me get familiar with the surroundings, the location, the size, and the detail. I can take all of this in before the lecture starts so I can factor these elements in as background 'noise'. This, to some extent, allows me to manage some of the surrounding information and to minimise the 'shutdowns'.

But I can't escape the crowds of students in the lecture theatre and I do tend to go into autopilot mode. For example, I might copy whatever the lecturer is doing or write down any notes that are put up on the projector or written on the board. Writing and listening are two very different modes, so I won't benefit from understanding the talk as I write. If I do manage to listen without writing, then there is a high risk that I will not always hear what is said. It feels very much like the sails or blades of a windmill as they pass. I will catch some detail, then it's blocked and then it's unblocked, and so on. I find myself connecting the dots much of the time and second guessing what is said in between the unblocked parts of the information I have heard. It's a very typical daily issue for me and one I have had to learn to cope with. So in lectures, I would miss important information that needed to be covered and would rely heavily on course notes and books to catch up on the content of the lecture.

How were your school placements organised as part of your teacher training?

Although the university offered support, I didn't like the unpredictable nature of waiting and seeing which schools would offer me a place, or when this would happen. As it was a two-year course, the placements were supposed to be spread over those two years. Therefore, I took the initiative to organise these placements myself. Very early in the course, I made a list of all the schools I wanted to train in and wrote dozens of letters. I knew exactly which schools I was happy to travel to, so that ticked one box.

The 'observation week' was in a primary school down the road from my home. This involved shadowing a primary school teacher during her typical week of teaching a class. After that, I used my network of contacts to get my first secondary school placement out of the way. The next two were in response to my letters. One was a Catholic school and the other a mixed state school for pupils aged 11–18, close to where I lived.

Which aspects of your school placements worked well? Why was this?

I had a lot of pleasant encounters with the staff at each school. One that stood out for me was with a Head teacher: for example, he asked me how my training was developing and showed a lot of interest in what I was doing. He even asked me if I had a designated prayer area for my daily prayers. I explained that it wasn't necessary as I didn't live far away. Nevertheless, he was quite shocked that there was no designated area in the school and so he immediately asked the Head of department to allocate a prayer area for me. I was bowled over by how determined he was to ensure I was supported fully.

The Head teacher was like this with all of his staff, as I witnessed daily. Each morning during the staff meetings he would come in and boom in his deep bellowing voice through the door that we were important and to come to him immediately if we needed support. Approachable leaders, in my opinion, are the crux of a great school. And this aspect of my school placement taught me a lovely lesson in leadership and the importance of approachability and inclusion.

Were there any aspects of your school placements that were less successful? Why was this?

There were very few negative experiences, although I did encounter some derogatory comments made against Muslims in the staffroom. For example, assumptions were made about my attitudes towards western clothing, simply because I was a Muslim. I blocked these comments out of my mind, as negativity sometimes impacted me in ways I couldn't always control. It took a lot of energy to try and achieve this, because otherwise my mind would close down and I would be unable to articulate my thoughts.

What were your experiences of entering the teaching profession?

Ahead of applying for positions, I read a lot to prepare myself. The *Times Education Forum* paper was very useful, and *The Insider's Guide for New Teachers* by Bubb (2003) was invaluable. I read that little book from cover to cover and even memorised bits of it.

Nevertheless, I was shocked at the reaction when I used a particular piece of advice from the book at the end of an interview for a teaching post, after I was offered the job. I was happy to learn that they had accepted me, but instead of replying with an adamant 'Yes, please!', I calmly recalled what I had learned from that little book. I accepted the post 'subject to satisfactory contract and salary', not knowing the impact that these words could have. The Head teacher seemed to panic and handed me the salary scale. I looked at it, not really comprehending what was happening. He asked me to choose where I wanted to start on the pay grade. He saw my hesitancy and offered to place me in the middle of the scale. Of course, at this point, I accepted immediately. So learning 'a script', on this occasion, had a positive outcome, but I realised later that my comment could have been misinterpreted as indicating a lack of enthusiasm for the job.

What advice would you give to an autistic person who was thinking of training to be a teacher?

To consider their own needs first. Once I was aware of what I wanted out of a course, I found it quite pleasant. Having as much control of the training process helped reduce much of my own anxieties. Choosing a course that suited my abilities really benefitted me and I would certainly advise anyone, not just autistic trainee teachers, but all trainees, to look at what is realistic for them and find a course that fits their lifestyle and learning patterns.

What advice would you give to professionals who run teacher training programmes, so they can be supportive of autistic trainees?

Teacher training programmes can be quite rigid, depending on the set-up of the institution. If that rigidity can be relaxed a lot more for autistic people, it would help enormously. This might include providing time to process information, as well as allowing some autonomy for the trainee teacher to manage their own learning and placements.

Sensory input and anxiety factors are two main areas to keep in mind when running these programmes. There may be others that affect autistic trainees that did not impact on me, so it is worth taking the time to ask as many autistic teachers as possible and get a fuller picture of their world and how they cope with it.

Teacher training is a mental challenge for some autistic trainees, which can be easily rectified if choice and time are given to students at the outset. For example, in my case, completing one placement, or all placements, before essays needed to be handed in, was vital.

Each person is very different and copes with things differently. Many of my coping mechanisms are automatic after years of learning what works and what doesn't, so even I might not be aware of them. Course organisers might find that autistic trainee teachers are learning as much about themselves as they are about their course. But when they do, they can thrive and excel in areas that they choose to specialise in.

Interview questions by Rebecca Wood

Reference

Bubb, S. (2003) *The Insider's Guide for New Teachers: Succeed in Training and Induction*. London and New York: Kogan Page.

PART 3

FACILITATING INCLUSION

Chapter 9

An Unusual Teacher

Elkie Kammer

Starting out: Training to be a teacher

I was very fortunate to get into teacher training in 1997 at Northern College after graduating from Aberdeen University. It certainly helped having a degree in Gaelic and having worked as a student tutor for a year. So, I embarked on the busiest year of my life.

My greatest difficulties at college resulted from misunderstandings based on my literal and unique way of thinking. This hadn't been a problem at university, but most teacher trainers I encountered were rather intolerant of neurodiversity, which often led to conflict that could have been avoided. I once took the initiative of finding my own rural school placement, as the course leader appeared to be too busy, only to be told off for not consulting with her.

In addition, my ideas about lessons and teaching styles were usually considered incorrect. For example, one assignment consisted of setting up ten lesson plans for teaching a P7 class (the last year in primary school in Scotland, for children aged 11–12) about the Second World War. It was the time of the Balkan Wars and I had some materials from a charity I was supporting, which included statements by children in the conflict zones. I thought it was a good idea to start with contemporary experiences of war as an introduction to the Second World War. However, I was told that this was not the way the topic was approached in Scotland and I had to re-write it the way it had been taught for the past decades. Fortunately, attitudes have changed markedly since then: during my studies for a Master's degree of Education in Inclusive Practice ten years later, I felt greatly valued – not despite, but because of, my different ways of seeing the world.

Experiences of supply teaching

When I graduated with a teaching degree in 1998, teaching posts were so rare that only four out of 54 graduates on our course were offered a job. So, I started my career as a supply teacher, for two-and-a-half years as a probationary teacher and another two-and-a-half years as a fully qualified teacher.

Supply teaching brought constant changes and uncertainty and the need to quickly adapt to whatever situation I found myself in. This is particularly difficult for Autistic people, who rely on predictability to avoid heightened anxiety. There were schools, especially in deprived areas, which welcomed me back again and again, as my different style of relating to the children enabled them to engage better, whereas other schools complained about my classroom management and interaction with pupils and staff.

I was genuinely glad to have work, not just for the income, but also for the love of teaching, and was mostly able to convey this positive attitude to my pupils. Once I was called to take a P7 class in the last week before Christmas.

'We dinnae [don't] work for supply teachers', some of the children let me know, putting their feet up on the table and slipping chewing gum between their teeth.

'Who's talking about work?' I replied, unpacking my Nativity candle machine. By the time I was getting my matches out, I had everybody's attention.

'We ain't allowed fire in school', one of the girls informed me.

'Then don't tell anyone', I countered while lighting the candles. Of course, I was careful not to set off the fire alarm! The heat made the blades go round, letting the shepherds and wise men march towards the newborn baby. I got my recorder out and asked what carols they knew.

'Jingle bells, batman smells…' someone shouted.

'Rudolph, the red-arsed reindeer…' someone else volunteered.

'Stop being rude!' another voice interrupted. Meanwhile I started playing *Oh Little Town of Bethlehem*. Suddenly everyone was quiet. I think the music and the candlelight transported them to a place they had never been. After playing a few more carols, I read them one of my stories. Nobody interrupted. I can't remember the rest of the day, only that I heard some of the pupils whispering about me when it was home time. 'She's not like a teacher. I don't mind her coming back.'

I never had a problem seeing the world from the children's point of view to the extent of entering their mind and experiencing the situation from their perspective. Since my Autistic mind doesn't accommodate hierarchies, I always tend to draw alongside them rather than set myself up as superior. With children like the ones in the example above, this has usually worked well. However, it didn't always go down well with other members of staff. One Head teacher told me off for making lessons too interesting (we had made Egyptian mummies out of modelling clay). Another time I was reprimanded for siding with a pupil who hadn't been able to hand in his homework and played truant when the Head teacher threatened him with detention. After all, his homework was at his dad's house, while that week he was staying with his mum. These days, there is more understanding generally of issues like that.

During those years I filled in hundreds of job applications for posts all over Scotland, and travelled to numerous interviews, but was never successful in gaining a permanent job. I was told I didn't advertise myself well enough and I always struggled to answer hypothetical questions, like the standard one: 'What would you do if one of your pupils threatened you with physical violence?' It's not that I hadn't experienced physical violence in schools, but my reaction always depends on the situation leading to the outburst. Every incident is different and has many variables. Once, for example, a boy known for his unpredictable acts of violence stood before me, weighing a metal object in his hands and asking: 'What would you do if I threw this at your head?' Without thinking, I answered: 'I would press my hand on my head to stem the blood flow.' Then I told him about an incident on a steep slope in the Alps, where someone higher up kicked a loose stone, which came hurtling towards me, narrowly missing my head. The boy never threw the metal object at me, but my colleagues, on hearing about it, told me that the boy had in fact wanted to know what I was going to do to *him* if he threw the object at me. Well, that hadn't occurred to me, but apparently my answer satisfied him sufficiently not to assault me.

Apart from my difficulties with job interviews, I also learned later that I had become too valuable as a supply teacher, since I was always ready to take any work, long-term or short-term, P1 to P7 (the primary years of school in Scotland, starting at age five), English or Gaelic medium, the most challenging classes, even in Special Units or Special Schools. As long as I could reach them on my bicycle, I was prepared to do my best. All in all, I taught in 42 different schools in Edinburgh during the first four years of my career, before moving to Inverness.

Finding a permanent post and facilitating inclusion

The way I finally got a permanent post was 'through the back door'. In a school, where I had often done supply work, the Head teacher offered me a temporary post, which after a year became permanent. This is the school where I am still teaching. It is indeed a very special school, not just to me. It is known well beyond the Scottish Highlands for its ethos of inclusion. Being inclusive doesn't stop with the children, but also includes the staff. So it wasn't difficult to reveal my diagnosis of Asperger Syndrome. Everybody knows – colleagues, pupils, parents and other professionals – and over the years I have gained a lot of respect for my 'insider knowledge'. It also helped being part of setting up the Autism Rights Group Highland (ARGH) and, together with our chairperson Kabie Brook, holding workshops about Autism for school staff and other professionals all over the Highlands. My book, *Discovering Who I Am* (Kammer 2007), has also contributed to being better understood. My colleagues now accept that I don't attend staff nights out or that I often walk about during staff meetings and need a quiet environment in order to participate in group discussions.

Although I spent my first six years as a class teacher, I entered the profession to make a difference for those who didn't fit the norm. Therefore, I was grateful when the opportunity arose to become a Learning Support Teacher, for which I completed the Master's of

Education in Inclusive Practice. At one point I was asked to set up an Autism Unit for children who couldn't cope within the mainstream classroom. Nowadays, in the mainstream schools in the Highlands I am familiar with, approximately 10 per cent of pupils have a diagnosis of Autism. In my experience, many of them are academically way ahead of their peers, while in their social and emotional development they are far behind. Then there are the sensory issues in the busy classrooms and the wider school, often leading to immense stress. Misunderstandings of peers and staff and the heightened anxiety created by unpredictable changes add to this. Understanding the problems from my own lived experience has made me their advocate.

In the beginning, I had four pupils permanently in the Unit, who had already been out of class for a whole year, working with a Personal Support Assistant (PSA) in the cloakroom or corridor, whenever they attended school. The Head teacher agreed that this was not inclusion. However, their anxiety and/or violence prevented them from joining their peers, even though the ultimate goal was to reintegrate them into their classes as much as possible. This implied a necessary change not just of the individual pupil, but of the class-room environment and management, which is where my work with the class teachers, the PSAs and the peer groups came in.

Many of the strategies laid out in the book *Inclusive Education for Autistic Children* (Wood 2019) confirmed my experience and the practice I have been advocating. The *Insight into Autism* workshops, held by Kabie Brook and myself, were geared towards enhancing the personal understanding of neurotypical staff for the ways Autistic people experience the world. Only such personal understanding can change attitudes and practice, thus making classrooms more inclusive. We also held workshops with the classes to enhance under-standing and tolerance amongst peers. Again, being on the Autistic spectrum myself makes what I say and demonstrate more credible. Sometimes I feel like an interpreter, translating between the Autistic and the neurotypical world.

The changes in attitudes and classroom practice have led to all of our Autistic children now being included with their peers at least for part of the day. Some of them still carry a Time-Out card and have their workstation set up in the Unit, though for some children this can be used as an easy escape from particular lessons they don't enjoy. Otherwise, they are timetabled for certain periods or specific lessons. For the older ones, I run Autism Discovery Groups, where we explore our specific needs and strengths, or study the lives of famous Autistic people, or topics like 'Friendships and Affection'.

Another important function of the Autism Unit is the Lunch Club. Children who cannot cope with the noise in the canteen, can eat their lunch with a PSA and myself in the Unit. Afterwards they can stay and play there or in the adjacent garden or relax in the sensory room attached to it. For many children, this is the only way they can manage the lunch hour and thus a full day at school. Some may say that this can lead to exclusion from their neurotypical peers, hindering the development of coping strategies for functioning in the wider world. The question of how much exposure to painful and/or anxiety inducing experiences Autistic children should be put under can only be answered on an individual basis.

Recently, major cuts in staffing made it necessary for me to take on a larger caseload, including children with other disabilities and educational needs. This has led to the Autism Base becoming a general Learning Support Base.

Ongoing issues

We have come a long way to make our school as inclusive as it is and I am often told that I am playing a major part in this. As I mentioned before, I feel valued not despite, but because of my own Autistic experience. This is not to say that I don't have problems and clashes at school. The sensory overload caused by visual and audio noise, strong smells and crowds sometimes makes me wish for a little cubby-hole to withdraw to, like my pupils do when it gets too much for them. The vast increase in electronic noise in the environment, due to the use of technology, causes me more and more stress. My literal thinking cannot keep up with the rapidly expanding computer language, and information overload often forces me to shut down. Misunderstandings still happen and can lead to confrontations. Although I am keen to socialise with my colleagues, I am aware of my shortcomings in this area.

Also, I have some strong opinions, which I can't let go of. One of them is my concern for children of high ability, either in all or specific academic and creative areas. Being employed as a Learning Support Teacher means that I am mainly involved with those who struggle in literacy and numeracy. However, many of our Autistic pupils are already fluent readers or gifted mathematicians when they enter P1, which resonates with my own experience as a child. The general attitude is to focus on their social development, whereas I believe we cannot speed this up. At the same time, we have a duty to cater for their academic needs, if we don't want to lose them to boredom or squander their gifts. So, I often have to negotiate with management and class teachers to give these children the academic challenge they crave.

I have never pursued a senior post, partly because of my struggle with interviews and partly due to my aversion to hierarchy. On the other hand, I am highly qualified and have decades of working experience and I am definitely amongst the 'seniors' in our school! Many people, but not all, acknowledge my expertise. Over the years I have had a number of confrontations with professionals higher up in the education department with regard to the practical aspects of inclusion. I remember times when targets for Autistic children included making eye contact, to stop rocking and flapping, to abandon their special interests and learn scripts of polite conversation. If Autistic adults hadn't spoken up about the effects of such practice and what was really needed to widen access, these detrimental targets would probably still be in place.

My stance against Pavlovian Conditioning (also known under the trademark *Make a Deal*™) and Desensitising has also sometimes clashed with the ideas of managers, who rolled out these methods as the latest protocol. Some people seem to feel threatened by the insider knowledge of Autistic adults, and fear that their position will be undermined. Perhaps they also fear the empowerment of Autistic pupils and the fact that they can no longer be treated as *deficient* and in need of *normalisation*. Many a time I attended an in-service day, or similar training led by non-Autistic people, where I couldn't hide my disagreement and was seen as disruptive. I assume this is one of many aspects that I have in common with my Autistic pupils.

Changes for the better and recommendations

However, I have also seen people's attitudes change. My involvement with the ARGH has given me the opportunity to influence local and national strategies, and I also have an advisory role in several Autism research projects. Over the years, I have been invited to speak at conferences organised by ARGH, the National Autistic Society (a UK-based charity) and Aberdeen University, the latter also seeking my contribution for a course in Autism as part of their teacher training. This in return has given me greater respect amongst many local professionals, though it will always be the case that not everyone agrees with me. The past years have seen a lot of change in education and in society as a whole, much of it being very positive and leading to better understanding and greater tolerance of people's differences.

To finish this chapter, I would like to outline some recommendations for making schools and the teaching profession more accessible for Autistic people. Compared to the significant number of Autistic pupils in mainstream education, there are very few Autistic staff. It is still difficult for Autistic adults to be accepted for teacher training or to be offered a post in a school setting (including as a PSA). I believe that the majority of teachers enter the profession because mainstream education has worked well for them. But with so many children who struggle in mainstream schools, we need more teachers whose own experience of education enables them to understand what changes are necessary to improve school for these children.

The specific characteristics of Autistic people should not be seen as an obstacle, but as an asset for schools and other educational institutions. The current reliance on formal interviews to select candidates for teacher training, teaching, or PSA posts, greatly disadvantages Autistic applicants, who can struggle with answering hypothetical questions and are often too honest to sell themselves well. Other methods of selection, for example offering a trial period, can be much more reliable in showing one's capabilities.

Most adaptations and allowances implemented for Autistic pupils are equally helpful for Autistic staff. First and foremost is the need for a change in attitude. As long as we expect everybody to behave, learn and socialise in the same way, we are bound to exclude those who are naturally different. To acknowledge and welcome difference is the necessary foundation for allowing everyone to be part of the whole and to develop a sense of belonging. Of course, there are standards of behaviour without which people cannot function together, but many idiosyncrasies associated with Autism are not at all harmful. In fact, behaviours like rocking, flapping, pacing, humming or stroking certain materials, serve an important function and are easy to tolerate. Clear, unambiguous instructions, routines and an altogether calmer school environment make life less stressful for all pupils and staff. Allowing withdrawal from a situation before it becomes overwhelming reduces confrontations. Acknowledging that equality does not mean everybody doing exactly the same enhances rather than diminishes participation. To illustrate this, I would like to finish with three examples from my current setting.

- For a school show in our gym hall, I put my ear defenders on like several of my pupils to mute the noise level.

- My colleagues are no longer offended when I refer to them as the P5 teacher or the PSA with the spiky hair, just as they do not tell children off who address them as 'Miss, Miss!' (even the male teachers), since they accept our difficulties with remembering their names.

- In the same way as my pupils are allowed to take their work to their desk in the Autism Base, I have the freedom to take away a new document and study it in a quiet place, feeding back my opinion later instead of having to take part in the busy discussion with my colleagues.

A few months ago, our area Educational Psychologist was leading a staff session about school ethos. One of my colleagues was still wearing his zebra costume, as it had been World Book Day, and with the Interactive White Board out of action (you can never rely on technology), we were writing and drawing on big pieces of old wallpaper. For a while I was lying on the table to ease the strain in my back and someone held the paper over my head, so I could see the pictures. It was a relaxed and joyful atmosphere, which kindled in me a grateful sense of belonging. In the end, we unanimously agreed on a school logo or mission statement. Then the visiting psychologist looked at us, slowly shaking her head: 'I've never come across a school like that', she mused, 'I can't give you any advice for improvement. Just keep up the ethos you have and share what you're doing with others.' I hope that by writing this chapter I can inspire more professionals to create truly inclusive schools. Unusual teachers, like unusual children, should be viewed as an asset for their unique contribution to education and ultimately to society.

References

Kammer, E. (2007) *Discovering Who I Am: Growing Up in the Sensory World of Asperger Syndrome.* Inverness: Brandon Press.

Wood, R. (2019) *Inclusive Education for Autistic Children: Helping Children and Young People to Learn and Flourish in the Classroom.* London and Philadelphia: Jessica Kingsley Publishers.

Chapter 10

Bridging the Gap

LIFE AS AN AUTISTIC SPECIAL EDUCATIONAL NEEDS ORGANISER

Joan McDonald

Introduction

Spending a large portion of my working life as an undiagnosed autistic teacher took its toll. Over the years, the energy required to work through sensory and social overwhelm, together with the annual flow of school life, finally led to burnout. This manifested as Chronic Fatigue Syndrome and led to me taking a career break from my permanent job as a Science teacher in a school for 12–18-year-olds in Ireland. A circuitous route ensued, involving work with disabled adults, then becoming one of Ireland's first Special Educational Needs Organisers (SENOs) and some years later, finding out that I was autistic myself. This winding career path finally led to my becoming the independent specialist teacher and trainer in autism that I am today.

However, this chapter concerns itself with my decade working as a SENO, spread over 80 small schools in the west of Ireland, in the years when additional supports for students with atypical learning styles were just beginning to be introduced. It was the first time that the health and education systems were asked to cooperate to such a degree. Parents' opinions were to be valued more, schools were to record specific adaptations in individual education plans and SENOs were to be granted access to classes and to school information – many new bridges to be built, and over uncharted waters! Although

I was unaware at that time of my own autistic neurology, reflection on those years leads me to recognise how my autistic thinking was beneficial to the role. This hindsight, coupled with my own current deepening understanding of autism, allows for consideration of ways to support and retain future autistic SENOs.

One of the first SENOs in Ireland

I was delighted to attain a position as one of the first SENOs in Ireland. This was almost 20 years ago, and the rights-based under-standing of disability and the practice of individualised planning for atypical learners was in its infancy in Ireland. New supports, intended to enhance the systems that had previously crushed individuals to fit convenient 'warehousing' educational provision were to be allocated, but with no real strategy as to how they would be used.

The job description of a SENO, set up under the Education for Persons with Special Educational Needs (EPSEN) Act (2004), was to support schools in preparing Individual Educational Plans (IEPs) for students with additional educational needs. A new level of cooperation between schools, families, health supports and SENOs was envisaged here. Having worked in three adult settings where person-centred planning was used, I was excited to be part of a more pupil-focused approach to learning for school-aged children.

The Disability Act (2005) followed. This led to an increase in the numbers of children being assessed as having special educational needs, and so a steady flow of health service reports requesting additional educational supports was guaranteed. Little did any of the SENOs know back then that EPSEN (2004), scheduled to be rolled out over five years, would never be fully implemented. Instead of supporting the development of creative, child-centred IEPs, our role in that decade became mainly as the gatekeeper of special needs staffing and resources in the schools in our area.

With an ever-increasing number of applications for support for special needs teachers (called 'resource teachers') and Special Needs Assistants (SNAs), and with schools concerned about the legal ramifications of writing IEPs, matters sometimes became quite contentious. A specific quantum of resource teaching hours would be allocated based on a label, rather than any defined actual need. This was aligned with the 'medical model' of disability, where the child was seen to be wrong in some way, instead of considering how the hours could be used to teach the way the child learned: in other words, adapting the environment to suit all learners, as is reflective of the 'social model' of disability.

A pre-requisite for employment was that SENOs had all worked directly with children with special needs. However, every decision had to stand up to the scrutiny of our managers, who often had no background in disability. We had outdated, inflexible public service circulars to work from, with scant information about how to apply them in real-world situations and no accountability as to how schools used the hours. Because it was assumed that the EPSEN Act (2004) would lead to new practices, management had little incentive to create detailed explanations around the existing documentation. Considerable empathy and diplomacy were therefore needed to explain this to parents and school staff.

My autistic skills in my work

I am someone who is passionate about everybody's equal right to an education. Autistic people tend to have highly focused attention: we notice detail that draws us in, so I became determined to find and understand every nuance of the system that pertained, to help me make fair decisions. I also have a tendency not to relax fully or feel properly confident in any situation until I have explored it forensically from all angles and have a feeling of competence: this seems to me to be an autistic quality. Secure knowledge is comforting and I can add to my concept base from there. However, while I familiarised myself with every detail and technicality in the circulars, it also became evident that there was a large degree of subjectivity needed in decision-making, as the circulars were not designed to cover the variety of situations we encountered. Even when Head Office staff provided short, clear, generic answers to our queries, there were always situations that didn't fit with the strict criteria.

Therefore, instead of ineffectively asking for answers to individual situations that never came, when I saw a circumstance where support was required, but it didn't fit our parameters, I developed my own routine. My approach involved creatively using the rules to get the best out of every situation for each pupil. This frequently necessitated an amount of negotiation with parents, schools and the therapists writing the report to ensure what was written down was sufficient to access resources. While I was first considered pedantic, people soon realised that I was not being awkward, but aiming to be helpful. This occurred at a time when people were very suspicious of SENOs and our powers, but with my approaches, over time relationships developed and people began to ring me pre-emptively to ensure we could work together on meeting the students' needs. My open manner and interest in fairness, while still working within the regulations, may have helped here. This ensured that any decisions I made were watertight and held up to later scrutiny.

Some examples of this occurred in the allocation of Special Needs Assistant support. SNAs were assigned specifically to 'address the special care needs of pupils with disabilities' where a pupil 'has a significant medical need for such assistance, a significant impairment of physical or sensory function or where their behaviour is such that they are a danger to themselves or to other pupils' (Department for Education and Science 2002, pp.1–2) and these parameters were applied rigidly. One very young pupil had a medical condition which needed close and frequent monitoring. As this child didn't fit the definition of 'disability', while clearly having medical needs, it was considered that the student did not qualify for SNA support. Having visited the school and received the detailed data I requested, I was convinced that the child's circumstances definitely warranted it. I wrote the paperwork, clearly and objectively, making it as compliant with the circular as possible and submitted it to management. The SNA was granted and the door was opened for future applications for such support to be made. I feel my attention to detail and ability to link creatively, but clearly, the child's needs to the criteria in the circular was effective here.

In these complex situations, teachers' and often family members' perceptions and records were crucial. Developing honest relationships and open communication with all parties involved really helped the decision-making process. Perhaps because I don't know how to behave in a distant 'professional' manner, parents tended to find me easy to relate to and to open up about their child's needs. Interestingly, parents told me they felt heard and understood by me, after almost invariably arriving tense and nervous for our first encounter.

A reflective approach

Autistic people are defined as having social difficulties. I can attest to the fact that although social structures and nuances don't tend to come instinctively to me, I have made the effort to cognitively work out what is happening and that has been of great benefit in all professional and personal relationships. While it could be hard to understand others' perspectives, reflecting on situations, actions, reactions and the attitudes behind them led to understanding of particular situations and added to my 'internal database' for future interactions.

At least having been a teacher, support worker and centre manager, as well as a sibling of an autistic man with high support needs, I already had a lot of groundwork done, as I had been in many of the positions of the people I encountered myself. I understood some of the parameters within which people in each role worked, pressures they might have been under and their expectations of the children in question.

At a time (approximately 2004–2014) when there was a wave of immigration to Ireland, parents from different cultures often seemed to open up to me. I suspect this was because we were both oblivious to the subtle local cultural aspects to social connectivity. Without that barrier, we simply wanted to ensure mutual understanding of the issues of concern for the pupil and to find the best solutions.

Although the dangerous trope about autistic people lacking empathy remains, many autistic people are very tuned in to atmospheres – how comfortable people are, the subtleties of how others may feel about subjects under discussion – even if we have difficulty working out the underlying causes. This perspicacity assisted in understanding the dynamics behind the somewhat artificial settings of planned and often very choreographed school visits. We tend to value authenticity while seeking the truth of students' actual needs beyond the school agendas of fear of scrutiny, staffing concerns, external pressures and fear of exposure of lack of knowledge about any particular disability. I had a strong sense of the atmosphere in any classroom and could generally tell when it was supportive and understanding. SNAs have an enormous influence on student well-being and inclusion. Through short observations and conversations, it was possible to get a good sense of how the SNAs engaged with the child, whether they fostered independence while assisting where needed or alternately perhaps if they smothered, de-skilled or overloaded the child. My own sense of the situation enabled me to offer useful suggestions.

Understanding and supporting autistic children

An indefinable connection often occurred with autistic pupils during school visits, even when not directly interviewing them. Given my sensitivity to atmosphere and energy, I could sense and respect students' emotional states and some of their sensory needs. I always respected their particular interests when they were evident. It was clear to me whether the children were in accepting, engaging environments, or if they were having their nature suppressed or were being overwhelmed by demand or sensory experiences. Probably my personal knowledge of being an outsider with my own struggles in education helped. Even before I knew about concepts such as 'monotropic' thinking (Murray, Lesser and Lawson 2005) and the anxiety of autistic students, adaptations made by supportive schools made complete sense to me.

Before the DSM-5 (a manual for mental health professionals which is used to describe autism) was issued in 2013, sensory sensitivities were not part of the diagnostic criteria for autism. However, half the pupils on my caseload were autistic and many had evident sensory needs. I could appreciate students' frustration levels as they were expected to learn in situations where it was impossible to concentrate. My own noise sensitivity caused problems both in school and the office at times. I would feel very uncomfortable in echoey classrooms and certain tones of voice would make it really hard to concentrate. In classrooms, I would almost jump out of my skin each time some teachers spoke. I also spent over half the week in a small office with one colleague, and could rarely concentrate when they were on the phone.

However, I also noticed that noises would disturb autistic children less when they were absorbed in a preferred activity, because there would be no tendrils of attention left to take in the annoying environment. I was able to share this knowledge with other teachers baffled by their students' apparently random sensitivities, which they might have mistakenly interpreted as being a means of task avoidance.

Most teachers at the start of this century had received little, if any, training in special education in their initial induction. As the number of autistic pupils in mainstream schools increased, teachers were concerned about their own lack of knowledge and how to offer support. Unfortunately, many of the new methods marketed for autism made teachers doubt their good instincts and think that pushing a child to complete a task while ignoring distress, or withholding the child's interests, would help them learn and indeed help their autism to become less obvious. It seems likely that this culture influenced attitudes to supporting autistic children even in teachers who had not undertaken training in these methods, and they may have felt under pressure to ascribe autistic distress as having no real meaning and to force the child into compliance. Therefore, common sense teaching methods involving supports such as visual scheduling, clear task breakdown, respecting sensory needs, engaging the child based on their interests may not have been used. These are helpful to all children, but essential to autistic learners.

Some unpleasant memories remain of this time where I had to speak out, although strictly speaking that was the role of school inspectors. The teachers were not deliberately cruel; they were doing what they understood was best for these apparently mysterious autistic children now in their classes. I found some incidents of forced compliance deeply distressing and discussed them with staff, to try to enable them to understand the children's perspectives and to consider more humane ways of supporting them. However, as I visited schools just once a year, there was little chance to follow up on any advice given.

Thankfully, understanding of autism has improved and more child-centred teaching is becoming the norm. However, compliance-based training has not gone away, and some teachers and parents still trust in it, not considering the potential long-term effects on the child.

In 2008, the NCSE (National Council for Special Education) funded my studies for a Master's degree in Autism, which I attained with distinction. The course gave words to some of the inchoate feelings I had had around classroom practices for autistic children and others with profound and complex needs. Rather than learning about particular teaching methodologies, the focus was on ethics, on the students' actual needs and on long-term outcomes. This sometimes jarred with the aims of schools that tended to focus on short-term goals or work towards state exams. The methods could be very damaging to the self-awareness and self-esteem of autistic learners who were forced to conform to something that they were not, and who had little autonomy. Therefore, the course gave me confidence to suggest more person-centred approaches to teaching each child when the opportunity arose.

My Master's degree was my introduction to an empowering view of autism. I met other autistic adults there and had an affinity with them, envying them their time in the quiet lunchroom and their interesting chats. It was to be a few more years before I realised that I was encountering my autistic kindred adults for the first time. However, although the actual concept of neurodiversity was still unknown to me, I was realising just how neurodivergent my own thinking was and also how I valued those schools and teachers who I could see embracing their atypical students and working with their learning styles. I really wanted to be part of that culture change.

School culture
In the 80 small schools dotted around the area I was working in, local ties were strong. Each school was its own microcosm, with its own specific and unique culture grounded in local community values. I

had to learn to understand and accept this diversity which impacted on the decision-making process. It meant that schools where students had the same level of need on paper could end up with different outcomes. Given my autistic learned habit of trying to fit into each situation encountered, I am used to trying to adapt. I noticed that often other SENOs, and indeed management, seemed to have an idealised vision of a school and could be frustrated with those who deviated from their expectations. I treated each school as its own unique social culture, and this affected some decisions I made, with different allocations being made for different circumstances. In these instances, it seems I engaged in more flexible thinking than my more neurotypical colleagues!

Work patterns

Most SENOs were originally teachers. I found the on-again, off-again routines of school term times difficult, even though I was exhausted by the end of term and needed a break. I preferred the SENO year which generally had a relatively steady flow to it. This was despite the fact that there were fewer holidays and that the work could be quite overwhelming at times. Mostly we could balance our work schedule between school visits and office time, so I was able to work to my own energy levels. This meant I could alternate school days with office days for social recovery and reflection on decisions. March to early June – resource allocation season – was completely exhausting, with demands for visits, responses to phone calls, paperwork and statistics to produce. But the rest of the year, one could make some effort to manage energy output.

In theory, on closing the office door in the evening, the working day was over, unlike teaching, where corrections and prep work could completely eat into term-time evenings. Nevertheless, for my analytical autistic mind, revisiting the discussions and observations of a school visit, or perhaps a phone call from a worried parent, cost many evenings and a lot of sleep in considering how to implement the best outcome. With experience, the number of such evenings lessened, but they were never completely absent.

Becoming a senior SENO

Senior SENO positions were created with a mixture of local management and continuing SENO duties, and I was delighted that the more outspoken SENOs, including me, were promoted. We might ordinarily be considered troublemakers, but we had a genuine interest in improving the systems to meet children's needs. Even though management brought a new set of expectations and challenges, I embraced the chance to cooperate more with our head office and with local disability service managers. Managing SENOs in neighbouring counties opened my eyes to differing practices that helped expand all our knowledge, and my forensic familiarity with our directives allowed me to incorporate alternate thinking into the whole team's practice.

My new role gave me an opportunity to deliver more presentations to other stakeholders, such as the Board of the NCSE, teacher and health organisations and local parent groups. After initial reticence, I discovered a love of giving such presentations: there were no interruptions, questions afterwards were about themes in which I was well-versed, and there was a sense that attitudes could really be changed with this face-to-face engagement. Formal meetings with other agencies were similarly stimulating. Our communication was bound by meeting agendas and our formal roles which suited my social engagement style. There was predictability, but also opportunity to advance ideas and cooperation.

There were downsides to being a senior SENO too. It entailed a lot more travel which I found exhausting: the concentration of driving or the sensory overload from taking public transport left little energy for the meeting at the end of the journey. Meetings of SENOs, initially occurring monthly, should have been professional catching up with valued colleagues. Unfortunately, I found it utterly exhausting chairing meetings with excitable SENOs bursting to share their work experiences, but also frequently degenerating into chats. I preferred the meetings to be more formal vessels of sharing professional information. The buzz and noise made it impossible for me to focus on the required topics. The resulting exhaustion meant I couldn't engage in the assigned time for casual conversations afterwards and could only work at half-par the following day.

Meetings of senior SENOs with management were even more difficult. As a national service, we were spread across the country, so we had to stay over in hotels whenever we met. So, socialising with each other in the evening and staying away from home were added to the demands. I'm a very social person, but the toll it takes on my energy is huge, and there was simply no respite.

An additional new challenge was that my reflective, over-thinking brain meant that I needed considerable thinking time on the myriad of queries that came my way from the SENOs I managed. Ultimately, with a combination of all of these factors, I could feel burnout coming on, so after little more than a year I abandoned the senior SENO position and reverted to my original SENO role.

However, even with this change, my work was getting much busier, with population growth combined with a boom-and-bust recession, and soon I was approaching burnout again. I requested part-time work with the NCSE. Sadly, that could not be accommodated. I stayed almost two years more, then resigned with no definite plans for the future, ultimately starting my own business, Posautive, that provides training and support for autistic people and those around them.

Conclusion

There were many aspects to being a SENO that I appreciated: the hundreds of families I helped, the schools that worked creatively and with a heart and a half to support the students, my SENO colleagues and the personal growth in disability awareness and politics afforded me by the role. I believe that autistic people have a lot to offer as SENOs, and I could have stayed if certain conditions had been in place.

During the Covid-19 pandemic, remote meetings became the norm, which would have allowed more contact without the travel and time costs of direct meetings. If this option had been available when I was working as a SENO, it would have prevented the energy drain of so much travelling and staying away from home. Hopefully, this practice can continue into the future for people who prefer it.

Neurodivergent SENOs, in particular, could benefit from having assigned time with a named mentor, especially for new tasks. As one of the first SENOs, I received quite an extensive induction, but that did not happen for later recruits. I also needed to connect with someone at a higher level in the organisation's hierarchy to get a proper feel about expectations and where things were going to avoid the element of surprise when work practices were updated. That accommodation would be useful for all SENOs, but especially those who are neurodivergent.

Another issue is that I shared an office. Although it was always helpful to talk things through with my lovely colleagues and hear their perspectives, on a sensory level, that was very difficult. The noise, smells and negotiations over office temperature that came with sharing space were challenging for me.

I could have stayed if my knowledge gained on my postgraduate studies had been harnessed. It seemed terribly wasteful for the organisation to have paid the bulk of my fees and allowed me study time, then not to use my skills. That became quite frustrating and was a major reason why I left. Other SENOs with particular skillsets had them utilised informally, but I felt the organisation as a whole suffered from treating SENOs as purely administrative workers, when on the ground we were offering so much more.

Overall, the role of SENO could be very suitable for an autistic person because it combines independent work with clear structures that have improved over the years. There is a good balance between visiting schools, making decisions and keeping paperwork up to date. Autistic insights into students' classroom experiences and into special education are invaluable, so autistic SENOs may bring unique perceptions to the work. I hope that, as time goes by, the public service as a whole will actively seek to recruit and support more neurodivergent thinkers for the unique commitment and insights we can bring to the education sector.

References

Department of Education and Science (2002) *Applications for Full- or Part-time Special Needs Assistant Support to Address the Special Care Needs of Children with Disabilities.* (Circular Sp.Ed. 07/02). Available at https://www.education.ie/en/Circulars-and-Forms/Archived-Circulars/Applications-for-Full-or-

Part-time-Special-Needs-Assistant-Support-to-Address-the-Special-Care-Needs-of-Children-with-Disabilities-.pdf. (Accessed 14/06/2021)

Disability Act (2005) Government of Ireland. Available at http://www.irishstatute-book.ie/eli/2005/act/14/enacted/en/html. (Accessed 14/06/2021)

Education for Persons with Special Educational Needs Act (2004) Government of Ireland. Available at: http://www.irishstatutebook.ie/eli/2004/act/30/enacted/en/html. (Accessed 14/06/2021)

Murray, D., Lesser, M. and Lawson, W. (2005) 'Attention, monotropism and the diagnostic criteria for autism.' *Autism*, 9(2): 139–156. https://doi.org/10.1177/1362361305051398.

Chapter 11

Working in Partnership

AN APPROACH THAT BENEFITS EVERYONE

Dr Ruth Moyse

It could be assumed that autistic pupils are best served by parents and professionals working in partnership together. Teachers do not go into the profession wanting to do any less than the best for their pupils; the nature of the role and the demands upon them mean that working in school is a vocation, not just a job. Parents, meanwhile, undoubtedly want their children to learn and to be happy in school. Common ground, surely? Yet, differences in parental and institutional attitudes and expectations (Wood 2019), as well as individual perceptions of a child and the way they experience school, mean the perspectives of each about how this can be achieved can vary enormously. As a result, working in partnership is seemingly far from commonplace, a perception that is supported by my experiences as a former teacher, a researcher into autism and girls, and a parent to an autistic daughter. This view is additionally informed by my work as a practitioner with the UK-based charity, Parenting Special Children, with families of autistic or otherwise neurodivergent children. This chapter will draw on these different experiences to explore the barriers and the benefits to working in collaboration from a UK perspective, and conclude by considering how the presence of autistic school staff can ameliorate or remove some of the challenges.

Arguably, the biggest barriers to working in partnership are the assumptions around desired outcomes. Or, more specifically, how to achieve them. Government, schools, individual teachers and parents may all hope for each child to be successful at school, yet success means different things to different people (Wood 2019). The current accountability measures of schools in England, for example, focus on exam performance (Department for Education [DfE] 2018; 2020a), underpinned by levels of attendance and conduct (DfE 2019; 2020b). In England and Wales, the Children and Families Act 2014 (Section 6 Part 3, para. 19) asserts that schools should help each child achieve the 'best possible educational and other outcomes', which tells us that positive outcomes at school should not be defined simply by the number of qualifications achieved but include other measures of success.

In either case, there is clear legal provision for the needs of autistic children to be met in school, in order to achieve positive outcomes. In the UK, the Equality Act (2010) provides that Local Authorities (LAs) and schools must 'have regard to' the Special Educational Needs and Disability (SEND) Code of Practice (Department for Education and Department of Health and Social Care, 2015, p.13) and that schools should make 'reasonable adjustments' (p.17) to address any special educational needs. In addition, the importance of involving parents in decisions about the services and support provided to their children is now recognised. One of the key recommendations from the Lamb Inquiry (2009, part of a response by the UK government to a House of Commons report on Special Educational Needs), was for schools to treat parents 'as equal partners with expertise in their children's needs', as such engagement can have 'a profound impact on children's progress' (p.4).

This all makes for some potential conflicts and tensions between home, school and the local authority. There may be problems if school and parents do not agree on the type of provision required by a child, what comprises a 'reasonable adjustment' or what best outcomes look like for the child. These are all issues that may well be avoided with input from autistic staff because of their insight as experts by experience (Wood and Happé 2021). Decisions around what provision is suitable may be led by what the school believes it can afford, rather than a child's needs, while parents may be prosecuted if their child does not attend school (DfE 2019), even if parents do not regard the school provision as suitable.

Moreover, while all parties may agree to a large extent that academic and vocational success at school are desirable, performance measures that encourage conformity and a uniformity of approach, perhaps resulting from the pressure to achieve, may also effectively result in the non-acceptance of difference. Even though a uniformity of approach may be designed to encourage a sense of community and belonging, difference by extension may be viewed as a deficit in need of correction, or an indicator that a child does not belong. This is problematic for autistic children and young people, who may struggle to survive an education system that is not designed to support neurodivergent pupils. It is also challenging for their parents (who may also be autistic), and for any autistic staff sharing the school environment.

This was evident from my doctoral research (Moyse 2021) with ten autistic girls who had stopped attending mainstream secondary schools. I found that an emphasis in school on uniformity and conformity was detrimental both to their education and to their mental health. As part of the research, the girls answered questions on nine themes about the sort of school they would not like to attend, and their ideal school (based on an exercise by Williams and Hanke 2007). All of the participants said they would least like to go to schools that they thought valued grades the most, which was surprising, as eight of the girls described themselves as academically able and had high aspirations for future careers. Their preference was for a school that would prioritise their well-being and treat them kindly; a place where they could be happy. Interestingly, when I asked them what was most important in their ideal school, the theme of 'adults' was selected most frequently. One reason for this is clearly explained by Rosie (not her real name), who said that school staff needed to know everything about her and understand her because if the adults 'don't know why they are doing things and agree with the reasons behind it, they just won't do it'.

The girls also created timelines of the most significant positive and negative events to them in their school histories, which they then analysed. An ethos emphasising conformity and uniformity appeared to mean that teachers were not able or prepared to respond to individual needs. Some of the girls described feeling like a burden in class, and most of them depicted multiple episodes of bullying by peers and sometimes by staff. The sensory impact of the environment, relentless pressure and strong feelings of being treated unjustly were also significant themes. The girls suggested that better staff understanding, and more supportive attitudes, would have helped reduce or prevent their negative experiences. These are all themes which have been revealed through our research into autistic teachers as part of the Autistic School Staff Project (Wood and Happé 2021).

For the girls in my doctoral study, a school that cared primarily for their well-being, that made them feel seen, safe and respected, was more desirable than one that prioritised academic achievement. They wanted to learn and tried to find opportunities to continue their education even after they stopped attending school, but found it difficult to identify alternative provision that offered a nurturing environment and fulfilled their academic needs. These girls did not reject learning, but rather a school ethos and an environment they experienced as damaging to them.

My research also found that while some current school performance indicators may identify some pupils who are struggling, they didn't detect the autistic girls in my study until too much damage had been done. Most of the autistic girls I met had been able to meet or exceed expected grades before their official attendance figures dropped substantially, which themselves hid multiple unrecorded or informal absences. Late acceptance of need meant the implementation of support measures at that point was less likely to result in a successful outcome for the girls, and that they had often experienced a decline in their mental health in the preceding years. As such, alternative flags of concern are needed. Central to this conversation must be the views and voices of autistic children and young people, and those of their parents or guardians. We must also consider whether a more evidently neurodivergent workforce in schools, who would potentially be more aware of these issues, would help avoid the issue of autistic girls passing under the radar.

However, having your voice heard at school as the parent of an autistic child is not always easy, as I have found personally and during my work with Parenting Special Children (PSC). Perhaps the first thing to note is that many parents I meet are able to articulate clearly the difficulties their daughters experience. Nevertheless, some parents report that schools are not receptive to the information they provide, and describe not being listened to or believed. One possible reason for this is that some teachers think they already have a secure understanding of autism. Senior teachers and local authority psychologists, for example, might genuinely believe they know all about autism, but in reality, have a poor and outdated understanding of autistic girls.

These differences in perceptions have been found in comparing parent and teacher (or educator) evaluations of their understanding and collaboration in educating autistic children (LaBarbera 2017). In this study, caregivers (parents, families or other carers) and teachers were asked to rate teachers' educational, family-centred and collaborative practices. Interestingly, teachers consistently rated themselves higher than they were rated by caregivers, with some statistically significant differences. For example, 94 per cent of teachers thought they took the initiative to establish effective partnerships with families, compared to 57 per cent of caregivers (LaBarbera 2017).

In this same study (LaBarbera 2017), other striking differences were found in how well teachers rated themselves on their practice, compared to how much lower they were rated by caregivers in some specific areas. These included how well they thought they advocated for an autistic child, provided helpful strategies, or understood an autistic pupil's specific learning needs. Teachers also rated more highly than parents the level of encouragement they gave to caregivers to be partners in decisions about their child's education. It is perhaps not surprising, then, that some schools already think they are doing the best for their autistic pupils, while failing to provide them with the support they need.

Some parents who have worked with PSC report that staff can make assumptions about their daughters, such as equating muteness or anxiety with limited intelligence, and may even remove support mechanisms if they misunderstand or do not appreciate the purpose they serve. Some parents are told their child should be more resilient, accompanied by advice to push them outside of their comfort zone and to get them to face their fears. This is unhelpful and suggests the responsibility for solutions to problems lies with the child, an attitude which the Autistic School Staff Project research suggests autistic school staff would be likely to counter.

Autistic children and young people who mask their difficulties or internalise distress at school may be overlooked by teachers. They may be perceived as ideal pupils, with no impact on the classroom and no unmet needs, with staff unaware of what they are actually experiencing or the extent of their struggle (Moyse 2021). In such circumstances, parents who describe a child's resulting meltdown, shutdown, or excessive fatigue at home later may not be believed or may be regarded as lacking in discipline (Moyse and Porter 2015). In my work with PSC, I regularly hear of parents of autistic children and young people being told to attend parenting courses or of being referred to social services, when a child's behaviour at home is not matched by their presentation in school.

Even when parents are believed, some school leaders might object to requests from external professionals as well as from parents, on the grounds that they do not know the benefits such requests may bring in school. As a result, it is a source of frustration to parents who describe relentless fighting to get support for their children's education, as per their rights, with their relationship with school often portrayed as a constant battle. These experiences are not uncommon (e.g., see Burke 2012), and yet may result in such parents referred to disparagingly in school as 'pushy' or 'difficult'. In such cases, required support may only be offered when the need becomes impossible to overlook, such as when attendance drops dramatically and at great cost to the child's education and mental health. Unfortunately, this can mean that not only does the current school placement break down, but that it is also a huge challenge to embark upon a new placement thereafter.

I believe that the breakdown of some placements could be avoided if schools worked with their parents in authentic collaboration from the start. LaBarbera (2017, p.37) refers to this as a 'family-driven paradigm', where 'schools understand that the family has expert knowledge' and thus are 'entitled and expected to contribute'. This may require teachers to be trained on how to communicate effectively with parents (Azad and Mandell 2016). Actively including parental involvement in all aspects of the children's education and acknowledging the key influence of parents on their children's lives – as is often the case at pre-school stage (Visković and Visnjic Jevtic 2017) – would underscore the importance of schools continuing to work in partnership with parents throughout a child's education journey.

When parents report that a school placement has worked for their child, they invariably mention the quality of their relationship with staff and the difference it made to working together for the benefit of the child. This relationship is sometimes initiated before the child starts at the school or is developed while they are there through positive two-way communication. Either way, schools that welcome parents in and create opportunities for them to share knowledge and insights are greatly valued by parents (Whitaker 2007). This results in parents feeling teachers have a much better understanding of their individual child, rather than one based on myths and stereotypes of autism. This interest and concern also contributes to an increase in a child's well-being, with parents reporting that their daughters thrive when they are surrounded by school staff who understand them. Evidence from the ASSP has also indicated that parents of autistic children can benefit when they are supported by autistic staff who feel able to be open about their diagnosis (Wood and Happé 2021).

These connections can lead to a teacher making extra efforts to collaborate with parents, which caregivers view as critical in the education of their child, and is known to improve social and academic outcomes (LaBarbera 2017). Sharing information enables an autistic child to be understood holistically, as an individual with their own strengths and interests (Hoy, Parsons and Kovshoff 2018). These aspects are seen by some parents as instrumental in their child's development and well-being at school. Having autistic school staff in leadership positions could be particularly beneficial for autistic children, as they can help shape school policy and create action, as well as influence and advise on the practice of others. In addition, they provide autistic children and young people with a positive role model, which is tremendously important for autistic children (Capozzi et al. 2019; Lawrence 2019).

Reading the contributions of the other autistic authors in this book, all of whom have worked or are still employed in the education of children and young people, it seems clear therefore that autistic school staff can be a huge benefit to schools. Many of the barriers and issues shared by parents of autistic children (and the young people themselves) could be removed or remediated if the experiences and understanding of autistic staff could be shared and learned from. The 'insider' knowledge and life experiences of autistic school staff may be particularly important for the care and support of autistic girls, many of whom internalise difficulties and are overlooked or misunderstood.

Autistic school staff already appreciate the impact of the sensory environment, the benefits of regular, honest communication between home and school, and the significance of building trust; aspects that research regularly finds are very important to parents of autistic children (Hebron and Bond 2017). If autistic school staff were more visible, then many more could be much-needed role models for autistic children. If they were encouraged to share their insights with colleagues in the knowledge that these contributions would be welcomed, not judged, then practice would improve, and acceptance would grow. If autistic school staff were valued and enabled, the benefits would be felt not just by the autistic community, but by everyone in school.

References

Azad, G. and Mandell, D.S. (2016) 'Concerns of parents and teachers of children with autism in elementary school.' *Autism, 20*(4): 435–441.

Burke, M.M. (2012) 'Examining family involvement in regular and special education: Lessons to be learned for both sides.' *International Review of Research in Developmental Disabilities, 43*: 187–218.

Capozzi, S., Barmache, D., Cladis, E., Vallejo Peña, E. and Kocur, J. (2019) 'The significance of involving non-speaking autistic peer mentors in educational programs.' *Autism in Adulthood, 1*(3): 170–172.

Children and Families Act 2014 (c. 6, 2014) Available at www.legislation.gov.uk/ukpga/2014/6/contents/enacted. (Accessed 15/04/2021)

Department for Education (2018) *Primary school accountability in 2019: Technical guide.* Available at https://assets.publishing.service.gov.uk/government/uploads/system/uploads/attachment_data/file/854515/Primary_school_accountability_in_2019_technical_guide_2_Dec_2019.pdf. (Accessed 29/03/2021)

Department for Education (2019) *A Guide to Absence Statistics.* Available at https://assets.publishing.service.gov.uk/government/uploads/system/uploads/attachment_data/file/787314/Guide_to_absence_statistics_21032019.pdf. (Accessed 31/03/2021)

Department for Education (2020a) *School and College Performance Measures.* Available at www.gov.uk/government/collections/school-and-college-performance-measures. (Accessed 31/03/2021)

Department for Education (2020b) *School attendance: Guidance for maintained schools, academies, independent schools and local authorities.* Available at https://

assets.publishing.service.gov.uk/government/uploads/system/uploads/attach-ment_data/file/907535/School_attendance_guidance_for_2020_to_2021_aca-demic_year.pdf. (Accessed 31/03/2021)

Department for Education and Department of Health and Social Care (2015) *Special educational needs and disability code of practice: 0 to 25 years.* Available at https://www.gov.uk/government/publications/send-code-of-practice-0-to-25 (Accessed 29/03/2021)

Equality Act (2010) United Kingdom. Available at www.legislation.gov.uk/ukpga/2010/15/contents. (Accessed 15/04/2021)

Hebron, J. and Bond, C. (2017) 'Developing mainstream resource provision for pupils with autism spectrum disorder: Parent and pupil perceptions.' *European Journal of Special Needs Education, 32*(4): 556–571.

Hoy, K., Parsons, S. and Kovshoff, H. (2018) 'Inclusive school practices supporting the primary to secondary transition for autistic children: pupil, teacher, and parental perspectives.' *Advances in Autism, 4*(4): 184–196. https://doi.org/10.1108/AIA-05-2018-0016.

LaBarbera, R. (2017) 'A comparison of teacher and caregiver perspectives of collaboration in the education of students with autism spectrum disorders.' *Teacher Education Quarterly, 44*(3): 35–56.

Lamb, B. (2009) *Lamb Inquiry: special educational needs and parental confidence: report to the Secretary of State on the Lamb Inquiry review of SEN and disability information.* Available at https://webarchive.nationalarchives.gov.uk/20130320215632/https:/www.education.gov.uk/publications/standard/publicationDetail/Page1/DCSF-01143-2009. (Accessed 31/03/2021)

Lawrence, C. (2019) '"I can be a role model for autistic pupils": Investigating the voice of the autistic teacher.' *Teacher Education Advancement Network Journal, 11*(2): 50–58.

Moyse, R. and Porter, J. (2015) 'The experience of the hidden curriculum for autistic girls at mainstream primary schools.' *European Journal of Special Needs Education, 30*(2): 187–201. https://doi.org/10.1080/08856257.2014.986915.

Moyse, R. (2021) 'Missing: The autistic girls absent from mainstream secondary schools.' PhD Thesis. University of Reading. Available at https://centaur.reading.ac.uk/97405. (Accessed 01/12/21)

Wood, R. and Happé, F. (2021) 'What are the views and experiences of autistic teachers? Findings from an online survey in the UK.' *Disability & Society.* https://doi.org/10.1080/09687599.2021.1916888.

Visković, I. and Visnjic Jevtic, A. (2017) 'Teachers' opinions on the possibilities of collaboration with parents.' *Croatian Journal of Education, 19*(1): 117 146. https://doi.org/10.15516/cje.v19i1.2049.

Whitaker, P. (2007) 'Provision for youngsters with autistic spectrum disorders in mainstream schools: What parents say — and what parents want.' *British Journal of Special Education, 34*(3): 170–178. https://doi.org/10.1111/j.1467-8578.2007.00473.x.

Williams, J. and Hanke, D. (2007) '"Do you know what sort of school I want?": Optimum features of school provision for pupils with autistic spectrum disorder.' *Good Autism Practice, 8*(2): 51–63.

Wood, R. (2019) *Inclusive Education for Autistic Children: Helping Children and Young People to Learn and Flourish in the Classroom.* London and Philadelphia: Jessica Kingsley Publishers.

Chapter 12

All About Us

LEARNING ABOUT BEING AUTISTIC FROM MY AUTISTIC PUPILS

Andrew Miller

Introduction

In this chapter, I will explore what more than 250 of my autistic pupils and I learned about our autism from a body of work that I carried out over an 11-year period. This was an aspect of my role as a specialist autism advisory teacher that involved me going into their schools to guide these pupils individually through a programme I was developing called 'All About Me' (Miller 2018). The programme was designed to introduce each pupil that was referred for it to their autism diagnosis and provide them with a personalised explanation of what being autistic might mean for them. On most occasions, this was the first time the pupils had ever been told that they were autistic.

Although the principal aim of the work was for me to support my pupils in beginning to accept being autistic into their self-identity, this chapter also focuses on how my views on autism, particularly in relation to myself, were shaped through listening to and observing their responses to various aspects of the programme.

My autistic identity and my teaching career

I had to wait until the age of 59 before I received my own clinical diagnosis of autism. It came four years after I had taken early retirement from my teaching career which had spanned 30 years. As well as being a class teacher and autism advisor, I held various senior leadership posts in schools. So my career may seem to have been successful to others, but it did not always feel that way to me on the inside. I had difficulty appreciating my achievements when they happened, mainly due to heightened anxieties and challenges with executive functioning. I now believe that my decision to take early retirement was triggered by autistic burnout, following many years of struggling to keep on top of things and simultaneously attempting to mask my difficulties from those around me.

There was no crossover point between my work in schools and the discovery of my autism diagnosis, so I never had the opportunity during my career to take on the identity of being an autistic teacher. Despite this, and because of my unexplained challenges throughout childhood, I always seemed to feel a sense of affinity towards my pupils with special needs, especially those who were autistic. This leads me to believe that my experiences offer an interesting example of how an autistic teacher and their autistic pupils can support each other, wittingly or unwittingly, in finding out about autism and how it impacts on them. This is despite the fact that my pupils and I all lacked conscious knowledge that we were involved in a two-way learning process due to the presumption that only the pupils were autistic. It was understandable that as I was their teacher, my pupils would be expected to learn about autism from me. But without realising it, I was gradually learning a great deal about myself – from them. It was my autistic pupils who inadvertently signposted me towards seeking a clinical assessment of my own, and helped prepare me to accept comfortably my subsequent diagnosis as being an integral part of my own self-identity.

The 'All About Me' programme

Guidance on how to deliver a programme designed for introducing autistic pupils to their diagnosis falls outside the scope of this chapter. However, a basic explanation of what the programme entails is important for contextualising everything written subsequently.

I started working on the programme in 2004, having been inspired by the work of earlier authors in the area of teaching school-aged children about being autistic (Gray 1996; Vermeulen 2000; Welton 2004a, 2004b). Since then it has been constantly evolved on the basis of reflective practice, a growth in the literature base and feedback from participating pupils and their adult supporters.

The programme is delivered individually to each participant over three sessions. By leading the work, I have the role of telling (or reminding) each pupil about their diagnosis and what it means. At least one of their parents sits in on the sessions to offer their child emotional support and share this potentially life-changing experience with them.

Initially, pupils are guided towards completing a template on a computer to create a unique printed and bound booklet containing a personalised and positive narrative that explores their personal attributes and information about being autistic. The finished booklet is presented to the pupil in the final session for them to keep afterwards as a visual reminder of the programme that they can be proud of, and for their parents and other key adults to continue using with them afterwards as a teaching aid.

The experiences of autistic pupils before their diagnosis

Most of the autistic pupils I worked with in secondary schools (for pupils aged 11–18) indicated that they had some awareness of being different from their classmates before they left primary school, aged 11. Therefore, prior to being told about their autism diagnosis, some pupils had already expressed a need to find out the cause of their differences. Some seemed distressed and frustrated by their challenges. They might ask questions about why they had few friends or why other pupils sometimes ignored, ridiculed or treated them in other unpleasant ways. As a result, some autistic young people genuinely believed that the unkind things others said about them were true. These comments were poignant to my own situation, since I had felt isolated and different from the first day I entered a classroom full of children as a five-year-old child.

Some pupils voiced concerns about standing out as being the only child struggling to cope in everyday situations at school like busy lessons, group work, walking in corridors, break-times, eating in the dining hall or sitting in assembly. Not knowing the real reason for their differences, some even applied their own negative labels to themselves. I have met many pupils who variously said that they had mistakenly thought that their challenges were down to them being a bad person, stupid or weird. A few even said they must have been suffering from some type of brain damage.

These perceptions corresponded strongly with my own childhood self-beliefs. Having read accounts by autistic adults of their childhood and reflecting on my personal experiences more recently, I realise that if the situation is allowed to continue, such negativity can have long-term harmful effects on an individual's emotional well-being and self-identity.

On a practical level, there have also been pupils who wanted to know why they were singled out for additional adult support, were sent out of class for intervention programmes or had appointments with professionals. I have had conversations with many pupils who said that they did not engage with their support, because they could not see any point to it, or felt embarrassed. In addition, not knowing about their autistic identity precluded pupils from fully taking up their statutory rights to be involved in meetings where key decisions were taken about what form their support should take.

The importance of autistic children understanding their diagnosis early

My experiences of autistic pupils discussing their diagnosis suggest that the earlier a pupil is told, the more likely successful emotional and psychological outcomes are. Most of the pupils I told accepted their diagnosis well or at least with a degree of indifference. The pupils who did express disappointment or seemed reluctant to talk about being autistic after I had told them, were mainly older pupils who had already encountered negative information about autism through their life experiences. In some instances, pupils told me that they had first learned about autism from the internet, movies or television programmes that negatively or sensationally characterised autism and autistic people before they were told that the diagnosis applied to them.

These conversations with my pupils – an approach that might not be possible with non-speaking autistic children – helped convince me that early disclosure would be beneficial in most cases, provided it was tailored to the pupils' levels of cognition. Difficulties in thinking flexibly can make it harder for autistic pupils to shift negative opinions once they are formed. I have found that discussing autism sensitively, as early as possible, offers pupils a more positive view of autism, and that this is likely to remain.

The value of drawing up a personal profile

The first part of the programme involves supporting each pupil to identify, list and explore their main personal attributes for inclusion in the narrative of their booklet. This was intended to provide pupils with accurate and positive descriptions of who they are, containing information about themselves that they could be proud of and which many of them were not aware of before. Involving young people in providing this information and its use in explaining how autism impacts on them, is intended to help empower them through developing a sense of pride and ownership of their diagnosis.

With prompting, pupils usually came up with lists of words to describe their own personalities which, when considered collectively, described the individual as being a good person who was valued by the supportive people around them. Experiences of helping pupils complete this task had a huge effect on how I regarded autistic pupils and autism as my career progressed.

Before initiating this work, one main reason why autistic pupils were referred to me for support was to help schools and families address behavioural problems that had already arisen. Hence any work that came next was likely to be problem-based. However, compiling these lists often led to the discovery and celebration of strengths that pupils did not realise they had, and that some adults and their classmates were unaware of them having too. Some pupils' strengths were also concealed by their challenges. Therefore, the positive insights that pupils provided about themselves as individuals, while having the space to do this activity in a supportive situation, reinforced my already firmly-held belief in the need to focus more on seeing each autistic pupil as a person of equal value, rather than a set of problems or puzzles to be solved.

Guiding pupils through this exercise transformed my appreciation of the potential of autistic pupils and encouraged me to look much further beyond what they might not be able to do. Maintaining a strong focus on their good points also helped counter the negative comments they may have heard about themselves and autism elsewhere and which they had already internalised into their self-identity. They were also more willing to accept support if they needed it. Moreover, sharing and enjoying this experience with countless autistic pupils across the entire school age range, encouraged me to see my autistic-self in a positive light when I received my own diagnosis.

I also learned to see how pupils could be encouraged to use the list of their challenges as a useful tool for including them more meaningfully in meetings where targets were set and key decisions were taken about their support and their future lives. Furthermore, these types of pupil outcomes helped me to face up to my own potentially lifelong difficulties more constructively, by regarding them as being challenges that I could hope to learn to live with better over time.

Presenting autism positively

Learning to make the right choices of language made a big difference in how well I was able to engage pupils in discussions about autism and when describing their differences and needs to others. Unfortunately, the most common criteria for diagnosing autism lean heavily on negative language which present it as 'a disorder'. This is done through the inclusion of terms such as 'failure', 'deficit' and 'impairment' to describe autism as being composed of sets of symptoms in the areas of social communication and interaction and processing information. When I first started teaching it, negative terms like these were more commonly used in autism parlance.

Some of my pupils reported coming across terms like these in reports about them written by professionals or they had heard them used by adults in meetings. A few concluded that if such words applied to them, then their differences must be down to them somehow being broken or sick. Their differences in cognition meant that in some cases, initial views like this proved hard to change.

However, the programme was intended to positively introduce pupils to being autistic. Therefore, what these pupils reported, combined with the growth of the neurodiversity movement, alerted me to the need to be extra vigilant in checking the written and verbal language I used during the programme and in making pupils aware of what being autistic does and does not mean. Pupils showed excitement or a sense of relief after finding out that being autistic did not mean that they were bad, sick or mentally ill, or that they could not live a happy and fulfilling life.

By using more positive language in the sessions, in their booklets and on a consistent basis in any conversations about autism in their daily lives, pupils were encouraged to be more accepting about being autistic. A strong emphasis was put on describing the problems inherent to autism as being areas in which they were different to non-autistic pupils, rather than lesser. Additionally, it was emphasised that their non-autistic classmates had just as many challenges when trying to interact, communicate, work and play with them. This was done to make the autistic pupils aware that the problems they had could have arisen from a shared lack of understanding.

Experiences of teaching my pupils to see being autistic as a series of reciprocal differences rather than deficits, combined with their responses to these discussions, provided me with a firm base to start developing an acceptance of my own diagnosis and explore its implications constructively. It also provided me with the confidence to be open about my diagnosis by giving me the language needed to explain my differences and needs in positive terms to the non-autistic people around me.

Informing autistic pupils that they are not alone

The vast majority of participating young people said in their feedback that their favourite part of the programme was browsing and discussing information and photographs of other autistic people. This was thought essential, as pupils often expressed concerns about being isolated and without friends.

The programme also enabled school staff to introduce them to other autistic pupils who knew about their diagnosis and attended their school. This led to some forming friendships with pupils similar to them and so, by extension, the children on the programme felt less isolated and were happier about themselves and school life in general. In turn, knowing about these pupils' experiences encouraged me later to accept an invitation to participate in a post-diagnostic adult support group and to seek out further opportunities to meet others like me.

Prior to starting the programme, many of my pupils had not realised that other people like them existed, so to also find out about autistic people who had achieved exceptionally well and had even become famous in specialist areas such as science, technology, music, acting and art, often came as a pleasant surprise. I also made sure that the discussion about other autistic people could happen almost immediately after they were told that they were autistic themselves.

Researching and discussing the achievements of notable autistic people with my pupils benefitted me by offering further proof that my areas of strength and past achievements could not preclude me from being identified as autistic. This helped banish doubts I had over whether to proceed with my clinical assessment after it was offered. I also reviewed more than 130 pupils' booklets as a retrospective work study for my Master's dissertation. Seeing the breadth of diversity amongst autistic people represented in this way made it even clearer to me that I should not rule out the possibility of being autistic myself, without at least undergoing an assessment.

All About Us

I am convinced that listening to what my autistic pupils had to say about themselves was key to me later being diagnosed as autistic myself. Throughout my life, I was constantly aware of being different and that some of my challenges and life experiences seemed similar to those described by autistic people. However, none of this seemed to quite add up enough for me to consider that I might actually be autistic myself, due mainly to what I had previously achieved. The ultimate realisation that I might be autistic after all came in a therapy session while I was talking about my experiences of being in unstructured social situations. It was a classic lightbulb moment in which it suddenly dawned on me that what I was saying resonated with what many of my autistic pupils had told me about themselves during the programme.

At that point I asked to be referred for a clinical assessment since I felt that I needed to find out one way or another in order to clarify who I really was. Clearly, besides my therapist and those carrying out the assessment, it is my autistic pupils who I have to thank for this life-changing event.

Likewise, it is my view that my enjoyable experiences of discussing autism positively with my pupils and the relationships I developed with them meant that when it was time for me to be told that I too was autistic, I was ready to accept it as welcome news. When I started to develop the programme, my original aim had been to put together an initiative for my autistic pupils. However, I would have been happy to have been guided through the programme myself if I had been the autistic child that it turned out I was all along. Even though I was their teacher, it was the autistic young people who had taught me how to understand myself.

References

Gray, C. (1996) 'Pictures of me: Introducing students with Asperger's syndrome to their talents, personality and diagnosis.' *The Morning News*, Fall edition. Available at https://carolgraysocialstories.com/wp-content/uploads/2015/10/Fall-1999-ISSUE.pdf. (Accessed 14/06/2021)

Miller, A. (2018) *All About Me: A Step-by-Step Guide to Telling Children and Young People on the Autism Spectrum About Their Diagnosis.* London: Jessica Kingsley Publishers.

Vermeulen, P. (2000) *I Am Special: Introducing Children and Young People to Their Autistic Disorder.* London: Jessica Kingsley Publishers.

Welton, J. (2004a) 'Sharing the diagnosis of Asperger syndrome with our son and his peers.' *Nottingham Regional Society for Children and Adults with Autism Conference.* Nottingham, March 2004.

Welton, J. (2004b) *Can I Tell You about Asperger Syndrome? A Guide for Friends and Family.* London: Jessica Kingsley Publishers.

PART 4

STRENGTHS AND LEADERSHIP

Chapter 13

Autistic Teachers

UTILISING THEIR STRENGTHS

Lucy Coward

Introduction

In this chapter, I will explore the ways in which the qualities of a good teacher and some typical autistic traits overlap. While the tendency has been (and in some respects, still is) to view autistic differences entirely as deficiencies, I would suggest that some of these differences can actually become advantages in a classroom context.

Imagine someone with depth of knowledge about a particular subject, and a passion for sharing it; imagine that they also have a keen eye for detail and an intuitive knack for spotting patterns, and then imagine all of this coupled with a high degree of commitment to a chosen activity or goal, and a strong sense of justice. Am I describing a good teacher, or an autistic adult?

This is not to say that every autistic adult, or even every good teacher, has this exact constellation of characteristics. After all, in the adage that has been attributed to Dr Stephen Shore: 'If you have met one person with autism, you have met one person with autism'. But the overlap between traits generally associated with autism, and the qualities of a good teacher, is much broader than might at first be imagined.

This was not something that I envisioned ten years ago, when I first found out about my autism diagnosis. Born in the early 1990s, I am part of the first generation to grow up at a time when childhood diagnosis of specific learning differences was becoming widespread, and special educational needs awareness and support began to be an expected part of a teacher's job. But even as recently as ten years ago, the prevailing narrative around autism was bleak, and the realisation that I had a diagnosis was a difficult one. I thought at the time that any difficulties in my relationships with others must be borne out of my 'faulty' social skills, that any success I could gain would have to be the result of a mammoth effort to overcome my deficiencies, and that the best I could hope to accomplish would be to achieve a seamless imitation of 'normality'. Autism, and any degree of personal or professional fulfilment or success, seemed mutually exclusive.

In retrospect, this was unjustified catastrophising, but a significant proportion of media reports into autism, and even commentary by medical and educational professionals, were catastrophising right along with me. Like many autistic people, I began to question the accuracy and justice of what were essentially negative value judgements about autistic people, gaining medical authority and becoming pervasive stereotypes. This is especially true given that popular judgements about autistic people such as the notion that they lack imagination or empathy tend to be based on older research (see Fletcher-Watson and Happé 2019, for a history of changes in autism research and attitudes). What has become increasingly clear in more recent research is that, given the right context and environment, the same traits identified as autistic 'deficits' could be perceived as strengths. One recent book, for example, argues that autistic people's facility for spotting patterns has been an important component of human scientific and technological advancement (Baron-Cohen 2020).

There is a common adage in teaching that 'if you judge a fish by its ability to climb a tree, it will live its whole life believing it is stupid'. This perfectly illustrates the importance of developing a model of autism in education that appreciates difference rather than simply focusing on perceived deficits. Teaching is about creating the conditions for student success, therefore teaching anyone anything is about recognising that some of their barriers to achievement are not intrinsic but contextual. I would argue that this is especially the case for autistic children and young people in schools, which is one clear argument for fostering the success of autistic teachers in order to utilise their experiences.

Why might an autistic person choose teaching?

I am a secondary school (for pupils aged 11–18) English teacher, which at first glance might seem like an unlikely career choice for an autistic person. First, teaching any age group is a highly social job, and at secondary level it can involve interacting with well over 100 individuals in the course of a single day. Second, it's a job that requires a varied set of social skills, including sufficient social perceptiveness to read situations quickly and respond effectively. Third, schools can be unfriendly sensory environments, with noise and crowding being inevitable.

However, there are other respects in which teaching is both appealing and suitable to a person on the autistic spectrum. A school is a highly structured environment with generally clear rules and routines. The power of having a timetable that is mostly fixed cannot be underestimated, as adjusting to new routines and unfamiliar surroundings typically takes longer, and requires more concentration and discomfort tolerance for autistic people than for others (Booth 2016). When I know from the beginning of my week which pupils I will be seeing, when and where, and what skills or topics I will be covering with them, and that my week will largely resemble the previous week and the next one, it frees up more of my attention and processing ability to deal with the inevitable variations (routine changes due to school trips or assessments, the need to adapt lesson planning to meet the needs of students, pastoral issues, etc.). I often think of the school week as being analogous to a 'theme and variations' structure in a piece of music. When the particularities of each repetition are based upon a recognisable theme, the intricacies of each variety become the interest. In the same way, the school week becomes reassuringly routine, and yet never tediously the same.

Classroom interaction is also more structured than most types of social interaction: the teacher has a clear objective, the pupils have certain expectations of the teacher, and there are mutually understood rules for how everyone is supposed to behave. All of these expectations are at least in principle meant to be clear, fair, and to facilitate learning, including ensuring that children feel safe and supported enough to learn. That many autistic people teach themselves how to manage social situations through 'scripts' and rehearsal is well documented (Russo 2018), and in some ways this is good preparation for teaching and classroom management. It can even be something of an equaliser at the start of a teaching career, when every new teacher must to some extent learn, develop and rely on 'scripts' for questioning and praising effectively, or for dealing with disruptive behaviour.

Autistic comedian Hannah Gadsby and others have observed that some autistic people find public speaking, acting or other forms of performance paradoxically easier than casual social conversation, because they have an element of rehearsal and control that completely unscripted social interactions lack (Limberg 2019). It is important to note that teaching differs from these in that there is the critical element of student interaction, and that children and teenagers are nothing if not inventive in finding ways to go 'off script'. However, strengths in the more rehearsed elements of classroom teaching can help offset the greater difficulty an autistic teacher may have in mastering the more spontaneous aspects. In addition, children and teenagers are in some respects bracingly (and at times hilariously) honest; they are less likely, for instance, to conceal boredom out of a sense of politeness. While this does not make them any less complex than adults, it does eliminate some of the guesswork involved in deducing another person's feelings or motives that even non-autistic people can struggle with.

While many people on the autistic spectrum have unhappy experiences at school (All Party Parliamentary Group on Autism [APPGA] 2017), it is almost a diagnostic criterion to enjoy learning in some form given the autistic tendency to cultivate intense or 'special' interests (Wood 2021). While this is something that has historically been construed negatively as socially limiting and therefore discouraged by parents and teachers (Attwood 1998), having 'special' interests is increasingly being recognised as a valid way for autistic individuals to connect with others and can even be a useful avenue to forming friendships (Wood 2021). Therefore, a career that involves communicating on a subject that they feel passionately about, and perhaps even inspiring the same enthusiasm in others, may be an attractive option for autistic individuals.

In addition, and most importantly, an autistic person might choose teaching because they want better outcomes for children, especially those that might be at a disadvantage or feel alienated within the current education system. A report produced by the APPGA in 2017 found that in England, less than half of autistic children surveyed were happy at school, less than half of teachers felt confident about supporting a child on the autism spectrum and autistic children were three times more likely to be excluded from school for a fixed period than children without any special educational needs. Inequalities and barriers to accessing education associated with poverty, ethnicity and other special educational needs are also extensively documented.

Autistic people often describe themselves as having a strong sense of justice (Jarrett 2014), and so the combination of this and their own experiences in the education system can provide a powerful incentive to tackle educational inequalities. The potential for autistic teachers to play a part in addressing educational inequalities is something that education researchers have recently begun to explore, especially the value of their knowledge and experience in informing approaches to supporting autistic children and young people in school (Wood 2019).

What autistic teachers can offer

At this point I should also note that I am drawing mainly on my own experiences when considering what autistic teachers can offer, as openly autistic teachers are still fairly unusual (Wood 2020), and the benefits that they can offer are likely to be as diverse as the individuals themselves. Just as effective accommodations for autistic staff are unlikely to be a 'one size fits all', the insights that autistic teachers may bring to their teaching practice will not be identical.

As I have mentioned previously, one respect in which teaching is a very compatible career with autism is that it requires subject knowledge and passion. The former is explicitly specified in teaching standards as defined by the Department for Education (2011), and the latter is implied in the mandate to 'promote a love of learning and children's intellectual curiosity' (p.11). In teaching, having a 'special' interest in a particular subject area can translate into the autistic teacher possessing deep subject knowledge and infectious enthusiasm, which is an advantage given the research linking teachers' enthusiasm to their effectiveness (Keller, Neumann and Fischer 2013) and to their students' level of intrinsic motivation (Patrick, Hisley and Kempler 2000). The autistic characteristic sometimes termed 'intense absorption' (Atwood 1998, p.11) in specific interests can be an advantage in the classroom, as it can engender patience and tolerance in situations that might be expected to cause boredom and frustration.

For instance, I am almost never bored teaching the rudiments and rules of sentence construction, no matter how many times I do it, as I enjoy the fact that developing a grasp of something systematic and rule-orientated can paradoxically facilitate greater spontaneity and creativity in language. I try to encourage my pupils to think of grammar and vocabulary as the building blocks for better ideas, rather than measures of accuracy or something learned by rote to satisfy a mark scheme. Similarly, I enjoy teaching Shakespeare even to children as young as 11, because I like helping pupils work past the perceived 'difficulty' and barrier of the language to access the overarching appeal of its storytelling. In this way, I am able to see how something that may seem very alien and challenging when they first encounter it, can become familiar to my pupils.

In these respects, 'special' interests and enthusiasm for their chosen field could make autistic teachers a valuable resource in curriculum development, as they may well enjoy and excel at detail-orientated tasks requiring research and imagination, such as writing schemes of work. At secondary level, their depth of subject knowledge could well make them an asset when it comes to devising lessons for 16–18 year-olds, or creating 'challenge' lessons or activities for particularly interested or motivated pupils.

Alternatively, the interests and knowledge of autistic teachers may run more to special educational needs, as well as theory and strategies for supporting students with SEND (Special Educational Needs and Disabilities). In this case, they may make committed and highly effective teachers for these pupils, especially as working with smaller classes is likely to play to an autistic teacher's strengths. Having a 'special' interest in education and education theory can also result in an autistic teacher being highly motivated to continue to improve and develop their practice. Therefore, getting involved in teaching and professional activities within their school and sharing developments in education research, may also be fruitful avenues for them, particularly as they advance in their career.

It is also important to mention the unique potential benefit autistic teachers could bring to informing SEND support for autistic and other neurodivergent students. Recent writing on autism and inclusion in education has touched on the importance of autistic people being represented in the teaching profession for this reason (Wood 2019), and teacher Fergus Murray provided an excellent demonstration of the valuable advice autistic teachers can provide in an article for the *Times Educational Supplement* (2019). However, while their insights into autistic children and young people are likely to be a valuable dimension of what autistic teachers can offer, this should not be considered the only benefit that they are able or likely to bring to their school and pupils.

Moreover, there are some important caveats here. First, any autistic teacher's experiences of education and of what works for them will have been shaped by more factors than their autism. Support that might have been helpful for an autistic adult of a particular gender, ethnicity and sociocultural background may not necessarily be equally helpful for an autistic child from a different context. Second, the principle of 'if you have met one autistic person, you have met one autistic person' is just as true for autistic people dealing with other autistic people as it is for non-autistic people dealing with autistic people. We do not automatically and intrinsically understand one another any more than non-autistic people always automatically and intrinsically understand one another. Therefore, it can be unhelpful to approach autistic teachers or adults as straightforward 'translators' of autistic students' behaviour. That having been said, as teachers, autistic people have the benefit of experience to draw upon, having survived the education system (and some of its failings with regard to neurodivergent people) the first time around, which can enable us to provide useful general insights on good practice, as well as to sometimes make intuitive leaps regarding individual students.

For example, I once had the idea of allowing autistic children the opportunity to take a 'tour' of a classroom and to meet their new teacher at a quiet time of the day before being expected to join a

new class. As an autistic person, I was able to understand why walking into a strange classroom with a different teacher and different
group of peers unprepared might be a significant barrier to an autistic
pupil, and to envision how to make it less demanding in terms of
cognitive load and anxiety. This has now been adopted as part of my
school's SEND department's training for new teachers. Similarly, I
have occasionally provided informal advice to colleagues on how to
talk to the parents of autistic children. Being autistic myself means
that I have relatively detailed knowledge of where to find accessible
and good quality advice and resources on autism, which I can then
suggest colleagues pass on to parents or to the autistic young people
themselves. Moreover, growing up as autistic at a time when it was
less well understood and arguably more stigmatised allows me to
anticipate some of the anxieties that autistic young people and their
families may be experiencing, and to assist colleagues in engaging
with these effectively.

In her book *Inclusive Education for Autistic Children*, Wood (2019,
p.186) posits the possibility of autistic teachers acting as 'autistic
role models' in schools. Although my colleagues are aware of my
diagnosis, the pupils are not. However, I do consider myself in some
respects visibly neurodivergent. In addition to being on the autism
spectrum, I am also dyspraxic, which is a common co-occurring
condition (Cassidy *et al.* 2016). I occasionally tell my pupils that I
could not ride a bicycle at all until I was 11, and still cannot do it safely
enough to ride on the road. I have found that talking about having
difficulties with an activity which the majority of my pupils mastered
more easily can be a useful leveller. This is because it demonstrates
that struggling with a particular skill or activity does not constitute
an overall lack of intelligence or an inability to succeed in other ways.

As Murray (2019) notes in their article on supporting autistic
students, autism (and other specific learning difficulties) tends to
be characterised by 'spiky profiles': marked disparities between
different skillsets. Treating examination results and performance
within a standard academic curriculum as the only meaningful
measure of ability can be both arbitrary and somewhat exclusionary
of people who 'underperform' as a result of their uneven skillset,
societal barriers or individual life circumstances. While preparing

students to succeed as well as possible within the existing parameters is important, I would argue that it is also important for educators to promote a more holistic view of 'ability' and 'intelligence' than exclusively what is measured by examination results. Neurodivergent visibility in the form of autistic teachers and those who have ADHD or specific learning difficulties could therefore be an important step towards a more effectively inclusive education system.

Creating the conditions for autistic teachers' success

It may seem simplistic, but I would suggest that the first step towards creating the conditions for autistic teachers' success is recognising that you could have an autistic colleague. Some of the most difficult and distressing situations for autistic teachers are created by leaders' and colleagues' assumptions that no autistic person could possibly be on their side of the staffroom door, much less teach effectively. In attempting to describe the conditions whereby an autistic teacher can succeed, in this chapter I am drawing heavily on positive experiences at my current school. For example, when I started working as a teacher, one of the first things that stood out to me was the culture of mutual support amongst the staff and the ways inclusive attitudes were fostered.

Accommodations are attitudinal as well as practical, and I believe that schools best support autistic staff members when they create an environment where inclusion is the default, as opposed to being limited to a few practical supports available only when staff ask for them. People with 'invisible' disabilities are unlikely to ask for what they need unless they feel that their needs matter, and that disclosing a disability or condition will not count against them in terms of other people's attitudes, their job security, or their prospects of advancement. Additionally, autism can present very differently in different individuals, therefore it is important that an autistic staff member has a voice in determining the support or accommodations they receive, rather than being restricted to a prescribed set of options.

I did not tell my colleagues at my current school that I was on the autism spectrum until I had been working there for a little over a year, and, when I did, it was the first time I had ever disclosed my diagnosis in a professional context. However, by the time I had told my colleagues, I had already received significant support. Two different teachers who had been managing me had noticed that I sometimes struggled to process verbal reminders or instructions (particularly when multitasking or in a noisy environment), and had started putting more of their instructions to me in written form via email. Neither was surprised when I told them that I was on the autism spectrum, but both had made the accommodation before I told them, simply because they had observed that I worked more effectively that way. One of these teachers had also already taken the time to help me keep my classroom tidy and organised, and to develop routines to manage this independently during a period when I was struggling. Again, my difficulty in keeping my classroom organised was framed as a support need and an area for development of my teaching practice (rather than being viewed as laziness or a lack of professionalism) before I actually disclosed my diagnosis. Therefore, I would suggest that autistic teachers are supported more effectively when the adaptations they are offered are based on their needs as individuals, rather than on any assumptions managers might make on the basis of a teacher's diagnosis.

As such, much of what I needed was already in place by the time I discussed my diagnosis with my colleagues. Although I have not since requested specific accommodations for sensory and processing difficulties, I have experienced consistently considerate behaviour from colleagues, such as the offer of a quiet space in which to work during a particularly busy time, or instances where someone has made the effort to notify me in advance of a change to routine. Additionally, colleagues' attitudes to occasions where I might appear flustered by a minor change to routine, or may need to take a moment to process something somebody has said, have been non-judgemental. This has the benefit of relieving me of the additional cognitive and emotional effort of having to always 'mask' my reactions in these situations for fear of being negatively perceived.

Another respect in which managers and school leadership can support autistic teaching staff is to set them up to succeed with the specific projects and responsibilities they are given. This kind of management is likely to be effective in getting the best out of autistic teachers, as it specifically focuses on individual strengths and interests when setting targets. Setting goals that enable autistic teachers to showcase what they are good at fosters confidence in developing other areas of their practice and in dealing with aspects of the job where they may feel less secure. Furthermore, this enables the school and pupils to gain the full benefit of the autistic teacher's more unusual skillset, or the original insight that they may bring to a particular project or initiative.

Dealing with areas of difficulty

In order to best utilise autistic teachers' strengths, it is worth considering a few potential areas of difficulty and the particular ways in which autistic teachers might deal with them. Behaviour management, for instance, may come less naturally to autistic teachers, especially at the beginning of their career. Again, this is not necessarily due the autistic teachers' 'deficits': autistic teachers are likely to be highly concerned with treating their pupils fairly, and may also take a strong analytical interest in understanding why a child or young person has behaved in a particular way. However, actively second guessing one's own 'fairness', or being able to analyse the possible factors behind an instance of pupil misbehaviour after the fact, are not particularly useful in dealing with a situation in the moment. Therefore, autistic teachers may require some additional support in learning to read pupil interactions quickly, as they are likely to be less intuitive in certain situations than their non-autistic colleagues.

Behaviour that challenges by children and young people is often, by its very nature, noisy, chaotic and fast moving, which can impede an autistic teacher's ability to process the situation and respond accordingly. Having a school behaviour policy that clearly outlines expectations of pupils, and that is implemented as even-handedly as possible across the school, can help, as it grounds behaviour management in a comprehensible system. However, no system of rules is going to be sufficiently sensitive and detailed to precisely cover every possible variant of pupil behaviour and its context. An autistic teacher may therefore find it helpful to have some opportunities to observe how more experienced teachers manage classes, or to accompany them on duty or on learning walks, particularly if the more experienced teacher is able to have a conversation with them about exactly how they dealt with any situations that arose. Simple, practical advice that focuses on positive ways to support behaviour such as 'greet students at the door at the beginning of your lesson', or 'make regular contact with home about children's successes and achievements' tends to be more helpful than more abstract comments such as 'build relationships with students', as an autistic teacher may not immediately intuit what this means in practical terms.

This is not to say that supporting an autistic teacher's behaviour management will be exclusively a matter of helping them to avoid pitfalls. Behaviour management is about much more than dealing with classroom disruption; it overlaps significantly with ensuring children's safety and well-being, and instilling the values needed to live in a community such as honesty, tolerance and consideration for others. Autistic teachers may be especially perceptive in realising that a quiet, compliant child is not necessarily a child who is coping. The links between autism and anxiety in children (van Steensel, Bögels and Perrin 2011), and the strain of 'masking' autistic traits and behaviours (Hull *et al.* 2017), are beginning to be better understood, and first-hand experience of these may make an autistic teacher more intuitive in spotting a 'well-behaved' child who is struggling. Conversely, personal experience might also make an autistic teacher more empathetic towards a pupil exhibiting behaviour that challenges (especially if the child has a special educational need or disability), and they may be particularly adept at talking through situations with the pupils and helping them to develop healthy coping strategies.

An autistic teacher is as likely as any other teacher to want to progress in their career, to take on additional responsibilities and apply for promotion. However, applying for a new role and transitioning into new responsibilities may present additional challenges for them in terms of self-confidence and navigating a new set of expectations. I would suggest that autistic teachers may be more likely to take on new responsibilities or apply for promotion if they feel that they clearly understand exactly what the new role will entail, as the prospect of unpredictability can be particularly stressful for us. It is therefore possible that an autistic teacher will ask a lot of questions about a new role before deciding to apply. Again, good relationships with colleagues and management are important here, so that the autistic teacher feels confident in investigating the new role and perhaps even discussing or observing what it will entail with a more senior colleague in advance of applying. The positive implications of this are that autistic teachers are likely to have given a great deal of thought to any prospective new role, and may therefore be logistically and emotionally very well-prepared to step into it should they be successful.

Conclusion

A staff and managerial culture where supportive responses to difficulty are the norm creates the inclusive environment key to supporting autistic staff members, and undoubtedly benefits everyone. Despite the fact that teachers usually lead lessons individually, teaching is increasingly becoming a team activity, as the skills required to ensure pupil learning and well-being are so diverse. On any given day, a secondary school teacher is likely to need to liaise with their subject department on academic and curriculum matters, with the pastoral team on issues of student behaviour and welfare, and with the SEND department. I would therefore suggest that effective schools tend to recognise that staff with a varied range of skills and personalities are required, and as a result view difference as an asset.

My purposes in writing this chapter have been firstly to demonstrate the advantages autistic teachers can offer their pupils and schools. As a highly social career, teaching goes against the grain of the stereotype of autistic people being inevitably unsociable and uninterested in other people. I have therefore attempted to challenge these stereotypes, and to point out how some autistic characteristics (particularly preference for routine and strong enthusiasm for subjects of interest) may actually make autistic people well-suited to teaching. I have aimed to demonstrate not just the skills, but the values that might inspire an autistic person into a career in education, specifically a sense of justice and empathy for children and young people facing disadvantages in education.

Moreover, I have attempted to illustrate how schools can support their autistic teachers and enable them to use their skills and strengths to maximum effect. The conditions that enable autistic teachers to flourish (a culture of mutual support amongst staff, imaginative and adaptable management, valuing of difference and diverse skillsets) ultimately benefit everyone. I therefore hope that I have demonstrated how accommodations can consist of good practice that is available to all, and not exclusively as an isolated set of protocols put in place for a member of staff with a known diagnosis. My further hope is that teachers and school leaders feel more confident in supporting autistic colleagues, and more assured of the advantages they can offer.

Finally, I view this chapter in some respects as a kind of template for the future. When I was of secondary school age, there was very little representation of autistic adults in work, and the representation that was available almost always featured autistic men in computing or technology careers. There were few relatable resources for a girl whose main interests were language and literature, and no public recognition that an autistic person could be a teacher. As a young adult, I was advised more than once by well-meaning people not to disclose my diagnosis for fear of the impact on my future career prospects, demonstrating the ongoing problem of stigma around autism. Going back to the generation before mine, participants in a study of recently diagnosed autistic people over the age of 50 (Stagg and Belcher 2019) described feeling like a 'bad person' or 'alien' growing up at a time when there was almost no public representation of autism at all. By sharing their experiences, autistic teachers can start to create a more positive future for the generation of autistic children and young people currently in school. They achieve this by challenging the stigma around autism and broadening the range of future careers wherein young autistic people can see themselves represented successfully. In this respect, supporting autistic teachers and utilising their strengths actively opens new possibilities for the next generation of autistic young people.

References

All Party Parliamentary Group on Autism. (2017) *Autism and Education in England 2017. A report by the All Party Parliamentary Group on Autism on how the education system in England works for children and young people on the autism spectrum.* Available at www.autism.org.uk/what-we-do/news/appg-on-autism-launch-education-inquiry. (Accessed 14/06/2021)

Attwood, T. (1998) *Asperger Syndrome: A Guide for Parents and Professionals.* London: Jessica Kingsley Publishers.

Baron-Cohen, S. (2020) *The Pattern Seekers: A New Theory of Human Invention.* London: Penguin Books.

Booth, J. (2016) *Autism Equality in the Workplace: Removing Barriers and Challenging Discrimination.* London: Jessica Kingsley Publishers.

Cassidy, S., Hannant, P., Tavassoli, T., Allison, C., Smith, P. and Baron-Cohen, S. (2016) 'Dyspraxia and autistic traits in adults with and without autism spectrum conditions.' *Molecular Autism, 7*(48). https://doi.org/10.1186/s13229-016-0112-x.

Department for Education (2011) Teachers' Standards. Available at www.gov.uk/government/publications/teachers-standards. (Accessed 14/06/2021)

Fletcher-Watson, S. and Happé, F. (2019) *Autism: A New Introduction to Psychological Theory and Current Debate.* London and New York: Routledge.

Hull, L., Petrides, K.V., Allison, C., Smith, P., Baron-Cohen, S., Lai, M.-C. and Mandy, W. (2017) '"Putting on my best normal": Social camouflaging in adults with autism spectrum conditions.' *Journal of Autism Developmental Disorders, 47*: 2519–2534. https://doi.org/10.1007/s10803-017-3166-5.

Jarrett, C. (2014) 'Autism – myth and reality.' *The Psychologist, 27*(10): 746–749.

Keller, M., Neumann, K. and Fischer, H.E. (2013) 'Teacher Enthusiasm and Student Learning.' In J. Hattie and E.M. Anderman (eds) *Educational Psychology Handbook Series. International Guide to Student Achievement.* London and New York: Routledge.

Limberg, J. (2019) 'Is my autism a superpower?' *The Guardian,* 3 November. Available at www.theguardian.com/society/2019/nov/03/is-autism-a-superpower-greta-thunberg-and-others-think-it-can-be. (Accessed 27/03/2021)

Murray, F. (2019) 'Autism tips for teachers – by an autistic teacher.' *The Times Educational Supplement,* 4 March. Available at www.tes.com/news/autism-tips-teachers-autistic-teacher. (Accessed 27/03/2021)

Patrick, B.C., Hisley, J. and Kempler, T. (2000) '"What's everybody so excited about?": The effects of teacher enthusiasm on student intrinsic motivation and vitality.' *The Journal of Experimental Education, 68*(3): 217–236. https://doi.org/10.1080/00220970009600093.

Russo, F. (2018) 'The struggles of women who mask their autism.' *The Atlantic,* 24 February. Available at www.theatlantic.com/health/archive/2018/02/women-camouflaging-autism/553901. (Accessed 27/03/2021)

Stagg, S.D. and Belcher, H. (2019) 'Living with autism without knowing: Receiving a diagnosis in later life.' *Health Psychology and Behavioural Medicine, 7*(1): 348–361. https://doi.org/10.1080/21642850.2019.1684920.

van Steensel, F.J.A., Bögels, S.M. and Perrin, S. (2011) 'Anxiety disorders in children and adolescents with autistic spectrum disorders: A meta-analysis.' *Clinical Child and Family Psychology Review, 14*(3): 302–317. https://doi.org/10.1007/S10567-011-0097-0.

Wood, R. (2019) *Inclusive Education for Autistic Children: Helping Children and Young People to Learn and Flourish in the Classroom.* London and Philadelphia: Jessica Kingsley Publishers.

Wood, R. (2020) *Pilot Survey of Autistic School Staff Who Work or Have Worked in an Education Role in Schools in the UK: Initial Summary Report.* University of East London repository. Available at https://repository.uel.ac.uk/item/87w2v. (Accessed 01/12/2021)

Wood, R. (2021) 'Autism, intense interests and support in school: From wasted efforts to shared understandings.' *Educational Review, 73*(1): 34–54.

Chapter 14

Navigating the Teaching Profession

Mica Jayne Coleman Jones

I've always wanted the world to be a better place for everyone; more equitable, happier and kinder. This desire to contribute to a world that celebrates fairness and individuality has, I believe, enabled me to progress quickly in my education career. In this chapter, I will explore some of the challenges I have encountered along the way, issues of diagnosis, and the positives I have brought to different roles in schools as an autistic woman. This is despite the fact that much of my career has taken place prior to my autism diagnosis, which I received in 2019.

I knew from a young age that there were groups of people who were excluded from society. I have also long held an interest in understanding autism, since my brother first received his diagnosis when I was a teenager. I adored my brother; I was fascinated with the things he found interesting and his unique way of interpreting life. However, I noticed that my friends did not understand him very well and would laugh at the way he talked, because his accent sounded American. I was also aware of how my brother did not seem to 'fit in' with the world around him, and I was curious about why this was. Years later, my sister received the same diagnosis. My fondest memories with her and my brother were times when I was able to make them laugh and comfort them in moments of distress. When an opportunity arose to teach in a special school, I took it with enthusiasm, with the hope that I could make a difference to other children like my sister and brother.

I hadn't planned to become a teacher. In 2009, while studying at college, a welfare officer had asked me what my dream job was. I recalled a supply teacher who had changed my experience of school for the better. She had taken the time to teach in a way that I found accessible, after I had spent so long feeling on the outside, looking in. I therefore decided to study teacher training at university. During my teacher training, there were sessions which were intended to provide a focus on SEND (Special Educational Needs and Disabilities), but on reflection they provided inadequate preparation for what should be inclusive education and person-centred planning.

An example of this is knowing how autistic children might experience the classroom environment. Nowadays, I use my personal experience of high sensitivity to background noise and classroom clutter to design spaces that are calming and purposeful, yet this was not something I learned about at university, where I did my teacher training. In fact, it was when I was using my own knowledge to renovate a classroom while in a supply position that I caught the attention of the Head teacher. He appointed me in my first permanent teaching post, with additional responsibility as Whole School Autism Provision Leader. This was the first autism-specific role at this school, and my first experience of leadership.

Sadly, my appointment was met with negativity from some of the older colleagues, who seemed surprised with the announcement, particularly as they were much more experienced and qualified than I was. In addition, and despite my best attempts to relate to others, I experienced exclusion by my colleagues at work. Based on interactions with me in the school corridors, I was considered to be blunt and to lack interest in others. The fact is though, that if someone had asked me about it, I might have confessed that long corridors make me feel highly anxious. In the past, I have pretended to be reading while moving from one room to another, just to avoid another social interaction 'failure'. I developed a strategy to keep my head down until shoes came into my peripheral vision, at which point I would look up and say 'hello' with a big smile on my face to avoid any further questions. I did not feel uninterested in others; I was simply exhausted by overthinking everything that appeared to come so easily to everyone else.

Although some relationships were problematic, the support of colleagues who were appreciative of my mission for change ensured that there were big improvements to the autism provision at the school. The day-to-day experience of pupils was improved by changes we made to the curriculum, the environment and staff approaches. Subsequently, the school received its first Autism Accreditation award from a UK-based charity, the National Autistic Society, and this encouraged me to apply for a senior leadership role at a large SEN school, as Head of Autism Research and Development. In part, I felt that I needed to start afresh as I continued to feel uncomfortable socially: I felt like I was excluded from colleagues' social circles, both in and out of school.

As my career has progressed, I have realised that some people value my style of interaction. I remember how one Head teacher called me with news of my appointment to her school. She said to me, 'Your skills lie with people and relationships, and my skills are in project management, and together I think we can change the world'. This was both inspiring and confusing to me. I had never considered relationships with people to be my strong point, although I generally find people fascinating. In a café, you will find me positioned in the back corner of a room, partly as a sensory strategy and also so that I can observe others around me. I just like to know how people interact with one another. I have had some special friendships with like-minded people, but I have also learned over the years that the maintenance of relationships with others can be exhausting.

I believe that methods of evaluating people's suitability for leadership roles are not always appropriate for autistic people. I almost always misinterpret the meaning of interview questions, or I consider the question to be contextual and can think of multiple answers, meaning that I cannot comfortably settle on one. This makes some interview strategies very difficult for me, such as when I was asked to complete a 40-minute questionnaire to determine whether my personality matched that of a school. On that occasion, it was also frustrating that I was never provided with any findings or conclusions from the exercise. I have since had to complete other seemingly nonsensical quizzes to determine my communication or leadership style, and while I have the impression that my colleagues enjoy these experiences, I find this type of activity maddening. There seem to be so many ideas on what leadership should look like, and I am yet to hear from an expert in the field who can describe leadership from an autism perspective.

As my career progressed, the expectation to speak publicly has become greater. This can feel both liberating and debilitating. In the early days of conference speaking and delivering staff training, I would call my family and friends with excitement. It seemed people wanted to hear what I had to say, and each event came with a bigger audience than the one before. After a while though, my rejoicing was replaced with heavy sighs, as I had learned that this also meant increased anxiety, which impacted on my sleep and eating habits. I realise now that presenting, for me, can be like a form of self-harm, but I do it because so much needs to change in our schools and society for autistic people.

Nevertheless, I can also feel a lot of joy when speaking publicly about something I feel passionately about. At a summer fair event, where I was invited to speak about girls and autism, I was surprised to find a friend and her father in the audience. At the end of the talk, my friend's father told me how well I did, and he seemed surprised that I could speak in front of an audience. I pointed out that presenting is far easier than a conversation, and I also got to talk about something I found highly interesting. I had delivered this presentation a few times, and I had learned that scripting my talks really helped me with surviving public speaking. I also use lots of visual prompts in my presentation, so that it reminds me of what to say next without needing to read from the slides. Since my autism diagnosis, which was in 2019, I have felt more empowered to publicly share what being autistic means to me, and I will now openly state when I am struggling to process a comment or question at an event, rather than making a botch job of appearing to understand and getting it wrong.

Another issue is how to deal with conversations. Prior to my autism diagnosis, I did not understand my inability to navigate group conversations. I would often feel perplexed in team meetings, would sometimes interrupt another person by accident, or misunderstand something said. I would then ruminate on these conversational errors for weeks, replaying scenes in my head and imagining better outcomes. Sometimes, I find meetings time-consuming because I spend a long time waiting for others to 'catch up' to my way of thinking. At other times I've been frustrated when I wasn't given enough time to express what I wanted to say, or I've struggled to find the right words and my idea was corrected, or knocked back, only for someone else to successfully articulate the same idea later on.

However, I have developed strong relationships with colleagues, and one I considered to be my best friend because she truly took the time to know me. At a time of bereavement, I had turned up at her front door, to be let in by her partner and, without saying a word, she sat me down on the sofa, sat directly behind me and gave me a bear hug, placing one hand on the top of my head and one hand on the front, and pushing down with just the right amount of pressure. I felt that we understood each other and I was able to connect to others with her mediation. In fact, she would jokingly introduce me as her 'autistic friend' long before I realised my true identity.

I enjoy meetings that are productive and follow a predetermined agenda. In the past, an unexpected invite to meet with a colleague or the Head teacher with no explanation as to the purpose had the potential to ruin my day. As a teacher or leader, the ability to manage unexpected events is an essential requirement, but a lack of clarity or clear communication should still be avoided. A clear agenda can help a person to prepare their thoughts on a subject, thus making the meeting much more productive. Nowadays, I rarely accept a meeting invite without first knowing the agenda. I know that I am not exempt from unexpected challenges, but I can respond to them differently now because of my developed sense of self.

I know some people working in education have held back from sharing their autism diagnosis with their employer or colleagues, either because they do not know what difference it would make, or they fear a negative response from others. I often find this out when people come up to talk to me after I have delivered some training. I have also been surprised by colleagues who have come to me to disclose their autism diagnosis, or their suspicions of being autistic. My first public disclosure of my own late diagnosis was during a weekly Girls' Club I ran at a school. I remain grateful to those pupils for their response, which was kind and incredibly mature. The disclosure opened a conversation about what it means to be autistic, and I felt a strong sense of acceptance and empowerment between the pupils in the room; each person was different in their characteristics, and yet united by their diagnosis.

There is an element of vulnerability that comes with disclosure, and it took me a while to feel unapologetic about the things that make me different. But the more I found greater confidence to say what my strengths were and what I found difficult, the more I was given the right support. However, I also found myself becoming increasingly exasperated with the uninformed views of others. For example, professionals think they know what autism 'looks like', and their ideas don't include someone like me. Because of this issue, it is unsurprising that there are autistic staff working in schools who have not disclosed their diagnosis to their line manager or colleagues (Wood 2020).

Overall, I have felt that disclosing my diagnosis has provided me with some legitimacy when making strategic and operational sugges-tions. At the time of writing, I work at a secondary special school as Leader of Specialist Provision. In this role and others, I have found that my autistic perspective is not only accepted, but encouraged. In my current team, we refer to this as having our 'spikes' (Carayol 2017, p.20), or inherent strengths, and we use these to respect and consider our different points of view. It is because of this empathy and empowerment that I look forward to every single school day, and I am able to contribute in ways that are helpful to the organisation. I believe that this is an example of 'neuroharmony' in action, where there is a shift from acceptance of difference to recognising how differences can contribute to a better whole (Vermeulen 2020).

On my journey to senior leadership, there have been times when I have felt frustrated, lonely, and outnumbered by the experiences and views of non-autistic colleagues. However, I have also felt a high level of satisfaction from working with understanding colleagues who, together, have enabled autistic children and young people to achieve their potential and enjoy their life. Being autistic has only been a hindrance to me when there has been a lack of understanding and reasonable adjustments. With this in mind, I hope in my future career, perhaps in a Headship role, to be able to design an inclusive school environment and invest time in staff, pupils and their families. My aim would be to identify what autistic pupils are good at and to create opportunities for them to contribute to a better school.

So, my thanks go to the empathetic colleagues and employers who have paid attention to my strengths, while forgiving my areas of weakness, and have nurtured my different points of view. In doing so, they have helped me to find a fulfilling role in education and a determination to influence a kinder society that recognises the strengths of autistic people.

References

Carayol, R. (2017) *Spike: What are you great at?* London: LID Publishing Ltd.

Vermeulen, P. (2020) *Peter Vermeulen on neuroharmony.* 4 November. Available at www.bing.com/videos/search?q=peter+vermeulen+neuroharmony&docid=607994148861463111&mid=0E3C0C009F82E59209F70E3C0C009F82E59209F7&view=detail&FORM=VIRE. (Accessed 29/03/21)

Wood, R. (2020) *Pilot Survey of Autistic School Staff Who Work or Have Worked in an Education Role in Schools in the UK: Initial Summary Report.* University of East London repository. Available at https://repository.uel.ac.uk/item/87w2v. (Accessed 01/12/2021)

Chapter 15

How Being Autistic Helps Me as a School Leader

A SOLUTION-FOCUSED APPROACH

Claire O'Neill

Introduction

Occupying a senior leadership role is not without difficulties, and, in my experience, being autistic not only amplifies these challenges, but also adds some unique complexities to the position. Nevertheless, autistic educators, given the right conditions, can bring unique skills to school leadership. Therefore, in this chapter, I will share with the reader my personal experiences of leading school communities. I will outline the unique skillset of an autistic leader, and by doing so, demonstrate why autistic teachers should consider and be deemed suitable for such an important position.

I have been teaching for over 20 years at primary, post-primary and teacher-educator levels in Ireland and have occupied a leadership role for much of this time. I am currently a deputy Principal Teacher in a school for children aged 4–13 in Cork, Ireland's second largest city. I am also the school's Special Educational Needs Coordinator (SENCo) and teach our Autism Class of six pupils. My daughter, who is also autistic, is a pupil in our school.

Before exploring my solution-focused approach, I will briefly discuss the challenges that being autistic brings to a school leadership role. The four main challenges that I have identified are: navigating and managing the school environment; the considerable workload; the effects of camouflaging; and trusting others with my diagnosis.

Environment

A busy school environment is likely to be challenging to most autistic individuals. Indeed, throughout my years of teaching, the bustling and dynamic nature of the school environment is the most common challenge voiced by my autistic pupils and their parents. This is not just the noise a busy school produces, but also the thronging and jostling crowds, the assault of odorous school lunches and the lurid and jarring colours often used in displays. A supportive and autism-aware school will make adaptations to the environment for autistic individuals. For this purpose, environmental audits to make school environments more autism-friendly are readily available online. Examples of these include the 'Sensory Checklist' produced by the charity AslAm (2018) and the 'Sensory Checklist for Schools' (Morewood 2021).

However, as a school leader, I am required to be in the thick of the school environment and be ready to cover additional supervision and dispersal times at a moment's notice. This can be an extreme sensory challenge. As this is a regular occurrence, I have to plan carefully for this as much as possible and have clear procedures for break-times, moving classes and dispersal times. Being in a small school, with approximately 100 pupils, certainly helps me as an autistic school leader, as the yard and corridors are quieter and less chaotic than in a larger school. I also find it essential to have a self-care strategy at particularly frantic times like Christmas and Sports Day. Again, a significant part of this involves careful planning and setting clear expectations.

Workload and multiple roles

Occupying multiple roles and having a complex workload is challenging for anyone, but particularly autistic individuals who may have difficulty prioritising and organising. In my experience, an ability to occupy multiple roles and an appetite for a multifaceted workload is core to being a successful school leader.

Therefore, I have learned strategies over the years to help me plan and prioritise my day. It is key to my success as an autistic school leader that I primarily keep learning and teaching and my role as class teacher as my core priorities. Communicating this clearly to others helps me significantly in performing my role effectively. For example, many administrative and planning tasks can be done far more efficiently at home in the evening. I also spend time prioritising tasks, and oftentimes I will give time to representing this visually as I find this reassuring and calming, and this practice ultimately leads to increased productivity.

These visual reminders are especially helpful when I am tempted to spend time on fine-grained policy tasks which I find deeply interesting. They also benefit my pupils, as they see an adult using visuals as a strategy to plan and prioritise their tasks.

Autistic camouflaging

Camouflaging, or masking, is when an autistic person consciously or unconsciously tries to hide their autistic traits, creates workarounds for what they are finding difficult, or tries to fit in socially with others (Pearson and Rose 2021). When masking, an autistic individual behaves in a more conventionally socially acceptable way, even though it would be more natural for them to behave in an autistic way. This process often requires immense energy and effort, and, as long-term masking is considered detrimental to well-being, it is thought to be a significant cause of autistic burnout (Pearson and Rose 2021).

In my early career, I certainly expended plenty of energy masking, often at a cost to my own well-being. I tried relentlessly to fit in socially with my colleagues. I was often baffled by staffroom dynamics and would spend too long ruminating over conversations and comments made by me and others. I frequently felt different, odd and on the periphery of the social life of the school community.

Now as a school leader, I find it a far more valuable use of my time to concentrate on the core features of my role, such as working in partnership with the Principal in leading teaching and learning, and building and maintaining positive professional relationships.

This means I have less energy and time to expend on conscious masking. The result is that I have a surer sense of self and increased self-confidence.

This change in attitude did not happen easily or overnight. There are several factors that helped me to mask less. For example, it is of huge benefit to me that my Principal knows that I am autistic and is very positive about my diagnosis. This means I feel no sense of pressure to mask with her and this makes our leadership relationship trust-based, efficient and positive.

Trusting others with my diagnosis

Nevertheless, trusting others with my autism diagnosis, particularly in the school community and wider educational sphere, is a challenge that occupies my thoughts and energy. I still feel anxious when discussing my diagnosis, as it requires so much trust in the individual this deeply personal information is being shared with. Fortunately, to date, my experiences of disclosing that I am autistic have been overwhelmingly positive and supportive and have only benefitted my school leadership role. However, I have been selective with whom I have disclosed to in my professional circle. At the point of writing this chapter, I have not disclosed to my wider school community.

I will now explain how I combine my autism-associated strengths and skills with a solution-focused approach to my role as deputy Principal. My autistic strengths include a sense of empathy, monotropism, the ability to place an emphasis on well-being and learned communication skills.

Empathy, particularly for autistic pupils

Unfortunately, for a range of reasons, there is a widespread and mistaken perception that autistic people lack empathy. However, one would not have to spend too long with autistic people to realise that they do indeed have empathy, and frequently feel this empathy intensely. Being autistic means that I can remember what it was like to be an autistic pupil and therefore understand the many challenges autistic pupils face daily. This enables me to empathise with my autistic pupils and helps me explain to others what the child may be feeling or experiencing at a given point in time. This serves me well as a school leader, as I can advocate strongly and effectively for our autistic pupils, and drive inclusive and supportive policies, plans and procedures in our school.

I know from personal experience the discomfort of a tight noose-hold collar or the steel-wool-like quality of school pinafores and trousers. I understand how deeply comforting it can be to have the security and sensory buffering of a hood in a busy classroom. Being autistic, I know that standing in a line can be extremely uncomfortable and one minute can feel like ten hours. I have experienced first-hand that school bells can be felt, not just heard, much like a torturous dentist's drill. As an autistic person, I understand why the lunchbox must be at a precise right angle to the desk and that an unexpected change of brand of crackers can lead to deep distress.

Therefore, as a school leader, I can encourage flexible and empathetic approaches to school uniforms and the environment and promote an understanding of these issues amongst colleagues. This empathy is helpful, not only for my pupils, but in building strong relationships with their parents too. Although I have never formally discussed my autism diagnosis with the parents in my school, they do know that I *get* or empathise deeply with their children, and this understanding of autistic pupils and their families makes me a better school leader.

Monotropism

The empathy I feel for my pupils largely comes from the lived experience of being autistic. However, it takes more than this to be an effective school leader. Another core feature of my autism that I consider as a strength is that if I become interested in something, it is not enough to have a brief brush with the topic by attending a CPD (Continuing Professional Development) course or by reading a single book or article. If something piques my interest, I need to know everything about it, from its origin to its application. This level of interest is very much like someone taking a clock apart piece-by-piece, cog-by-cog, and then painstakingly putting it back together again and not stopping until it keeps perfect time. In the context of autism, this quality of interest is sometimes called a 'special interest', an 'obsession' or, a term I find to be less judgemental and therefore more positive, 'monotropism' (Murray, Lesser and Lawson 2005).

This is almost certainly why I am studying for my fifth post-graduate qualification in education! The topics that have attracted my interest are diverse and include literacy – especially promoting reading comprehension and the writing process – self-regulation techniques and supports, and special and inclusive education.

This can be a very useful and even, dare I say, a necessary trait in a school leader. For instance, this level of interest means that I have a deep knowledge of several education-related areas. Such qualities are important in a school leader, as the school community looks to their Principal and deputy Principal as lead learners.

First cousins to the development of expertise in my arsenal of autism-related strengths and skills are deep focus and attention to detail. These traits are very helpful in a leadership role, as there are so many planning and administrative duties that require a careful and methodical approach.

For example, one of my roles as a school leader is that of SENCo. This involves reading detailed reports and summarising and inter-preting them to form effective pupil support plans. Oftentimes these reports recommend that the school applies for further supports for the pupil and this involves the careful and precise completion of official forms. My autism-related abilities of having deep focus and attention to detail means that I complete these forms efficiently and accurately. Ultimately, by being successful at using my focus and attention, our pupils have support plans that are highly individual-ised and suitable for supporting their learning.

Well-being

One enduring interest that benefits me as a school leader and deserves special attention is school community well-being. This is an area that is essential for any school leader to promote, nurture and model. There are numerous studies into the quality of life of autistic adults, including their physical and mental health, that convince me that self-care and well-being must be an integral part of my leadership role if it is to be sustainable for me.

Well-being is certainly one of my passionate interests, so much so that I took a secondment a few years ago to become a health and well-being advisor with our national Professional Development and Support Service for Teachers (PDST). Through this, I employed several frameworks that are available here in Ireland to support well-being in our schools. Now, as a school leader, I use these frameworks to keep well-being at the forefront of our school improvement planning. A healthy working environment is a huge protective factor for the health of autistic teachers and pupils. In my experience, promoting a positive school culture and climate is essential for an autistic teacher to thrive.

As a school leader, I can drive well-being programmes that help build resilience and promote good physical and mental health in our pupils. I only wish some of these programmes had been available to me as a young autistic pupil. Approaches like Positive Psychology Interventions (PPIs), which can be used to explore character strengths, as well as mindfulness and adapted Cognitive Behavioural Therapy (CBT) approaches, can have a significant impact on the well-being of the school community.

It goes without saying that these approaches form part of my personal self-care plan, a plan I would argue is helpful for all school leaders, but essential for the autistic school leader.

Communication

Communication is not an area typically considered a strength in an autistic person. Indeed, social communication difficulties are identified as a core feature of autism and social communication programmes are the cornerstone of many support plans for autistic pupils. However, I would argue that the ability to communicate effectively is a strength I have worked consistently to develop, and now consider a key skill that I possess as an autistic school leader.

Certainly in my younger years, social communication was very difficult for me. Indeed, I was considered a shy and socially awkward child, teenager and young adult. Initially as a school leader,

I experienced frequent communication breakdowns, particularly with colleagues but, thankfully, rarely with pupils or parents. These communication difficulties did at times make me doubt my abilities and meant that some leadership responsibilities were stressful to deal with.

However, I believe that being autistic has taught me to take a solution-focused approach to situations I find challenging and therefore I have placed a considerable amount of energy into improving communication with others, especially in a professional setting. A simple example of this is clearly delineating my preferred communication channels. This includes making it explicit that I prefer email to phone calls, and face-to-face meetings to video or phone meetings. I regularly check for understanding, both my own and that of my communication partner. I generally action items discussed and put a time frame on these actions. These approaches have been invaluable to developing my capacity as an effective leader.

An example of professional development I have undertaken in communication includes training and active practice as a coach. Effective coaching requires keen active listening skills, and how one can develop listening skills is made very explicit in coaching training and supervision. Similarly, a branch of mindfulness known as 'Insight Dialogue', which involves the interpersonal use of mindfulness, has helped me enormously in developing strong communication skills and conflict resolution.

Recent and emerging research suggests that the responsibility to correct communication breakdowns between autistic people and non-autistic people is not the sole responsibility of the autistic person (Milton 2012). Therefore, a whole school project I believe has great potential to aid communication in my school community is the introduction of Restorative Practices (RPs). At the centre of this practice are very explicit structures to support and facilitate effective and respectful communication and conflict resolution. I am confident that this will give the members of our school community a relationship-based and respectful means of communicating with each other, and a structure to manage conflict when it arises.

Conclusion

Writing this chapter has given me the opportunity to reflect on my career as a school leader, and it is clear to me that there have been several factors that have helped me flourish in educational leadership roles. I recognise that I am deeply fortunate to have a loving family who accept and support me in pursuing a demanding career. Furthermore, I have worked in schools that celebrate inclusion and diversity with very talented and dedicated school staff. I have benefitted from having strong and generous educational leaders as mentors and colleagues.

Over my 20 years of teaching it has been a true privilege to teach and support many autistic pupils and their families. All of these relationships have helped shape me into a strong autistic school leader. I hope that by sharing my experiences, more autistic teachers may consider and be encouraged to take on senior roles in education. I also hope that non-autistic readers will gain a deeper understanding of the valuable skills autistic leaders can bring to a truly inclusive and diverse school community.

My experience demonstrates that being autistic equips people with many skills that are relevant to being a successful school leader. Of course, there are challenges, but this is true of any position of responsibility and trust. However, with the right conditions, adaptations and supportive relationships, autistic people can thrive and flourish in leadership positions in education. Therefore projects like the Autistic School Staff Project are important and should be supported and engaged with by all stakeholders in education.

References

AsIAm (2018) *Sensory Checklist*. Available at https://asiam.ie/check-sensory-checklist-tool. (Accessed 16/02/2021)

Morewood, G. (2021) *Sensory Checklist for Schools*. Available at www.gdmorewood.com/resources. (Accessed 16/02/2021)

Murray, D., Lesser, M. and Lawson, W. (2005) 'Attention, monotropism and the diagnostic criteria for autism.' *Autism*, 9(2): 139–156. https://doi.org/10.1177/1362361305051398.

Milton, D.E.M. (2012) 'On the ontological status of autism: The "double empathy problem".' *Disability & Society*, 27(6): 883–887. https://doi.org/10.1080/0968759 9.2012.710008

Pearson, A. and Rose, K. (2021) 'A conceptual analysis of autistic masking: Understanding the narrative of stigma and the illusion of choice.' *Autism in Adulthood*, 3(1): 52–60. http://doi.org/10.1089/aut.2020.0043.

Biographies

Editorial team
Dr Rebecca Wood, lead editor

Dr Rebecca Wood is a Senior Lecturer in Special Education at the University of East London and a former teacher and autism education practitioner. She completed her PhD at the University of Birmingham, funded by a full-time scholarship, where she was also Project Manager of the European Transform Autism Education project. Rebecca subsequently undertook an ESRC postdoctoral Research Fellowship at King's College London, mentored by Professor Francesca Happé CBE. The Autistic School Staff Project was initially developed during this time. Rebecca's first book, *Inclusive Education for Autistic Children*, is also published by Jessica Kingsley Publishers.

Dr Laura Crane

Dr Laura Crane is an Associate Professor at University College London's Institute of Education, where she is deputy Director of the Centre for Research in Autism and Education (CRAE). Laura's research focuses on understanding the educational experiences of autistic children and young people (in mainstream and special schools) and identifying evidence-based ways to support pupils, their parents and school staff. Laura is also an expert in participatory research (i.e., conducting research with – as opposed to on, about or for – autistic people and their allies). Laura joined the Autistic School Staff Project team in 2020.

Professor Francesca Happé

Francesca Happé is Professor of Cognitive Neuroscience at King's College London. Her research focuses on autism. She has explored social understanding and 'mentalising' difficulties in autism, as well as abilities and assets in relation to detail-focused cognitive style. Her recent work focuses on mental health, and under-researched subgroups including women and the elderly. She is a Fellow of the British Academy and Academy of Medical Sciences, past-President of the International Society for Autism Research, and has received the Royal Society Rosalind Franklin Award, the British Psychological Society Spearman Medal and President's Award, and a CBE for services to the study of autism.

Alan Morrison

Alan first became aware of autism when he was studying for a university degree in Philosophy and Psychology, and like many others, spent many hours researching autism. He thus self-identified (as contemporary parlance would have it) as autistic, thereafter gaining 'official' recognition via the National Health Service in the UK. Finding autism to be quite fascinating, he has utilised his autistic perspective on life while being a school teacher, as a union member supporting other autistic colleagues, as a participant in university studies, as a member of an autism rights group and generally within society as an ordinary member of the public.

Dr Ruth Moyse

Dr Ruth Moyse trained initially as a primary school teacher and taught in the UK and internationally. She was diagnosed as autistic in her forties and subsequently developed a career as a researcher into the educational experiences of autistic girls and young women. Ruth is a Research Assistant on the Autistic School Staff Project and a Visiting Fellow with the Autism Community Research Network at the University of Southampton. She has also worked for the charity Parenting Special Children since 2013, where she writes and presents workshops for autistic girls and young women, their families and the school staff who work with them.

Non-editorial contributors
Mica Jayne Coleman Jones

Mica has used her personal understanding of Autism to make positive systemic changes in special and mainstream settings, and has delivered Autism training at local, regional, national and international events. On Mica's journey from understanding her siblings' diagnosis of Autism to her own self-discovery, she has worked in a number of educational roles, from newly qualified teacher to senior leadership, including Head of Autism Research and Development and Leader of Specialist Provision. In 2017, Mica self-identified as autistic, but later sought, and received, a formal diagnosis after experiencing multiple difficulties in the workplace.

Lucy Coward
Lucy Coward is an English teacher who has worked predominantly in state schools since gaining her Post Graduate Certificate in Education in 2014, teaching pupils aged 11–18. She was diagnosed with Asperger Syndrome at the age of four and is also diagnosed as dyspraxic. Experience of her own differences growing up helped to spark her interest in the different ways in which people learn, and different varieties of intelligence and ability. She enjoys the way in which teaching involves ongoing learning and adaptation, and the opportunity it gives her to share her interests in language and literature.

Elkie Kammer
Elkie Kammer grew up in Germany and Ireland and has lived in Scotland for the past 30 years. She left school at the age of 15 and trained as a gardener, eking out a living on organic farms for many years. Later she gained her Highers and a university degree and became a teacher. She received a diagnosis of Asperger Syndrome in her forties and now works as a Learning Support Teacher in Inverness. She is also one of the founders and committee members of the Autism Rights Group Highland (ARGH). She is the author of over 40 books, published in several languages.

Joan McDonald
Joan is a second level science teacher in Ireland, working as 'Posautive', with autistic students who cannot attend school full time. Following many years of classroom teaching, Joan worked in centres for adults with learning disabilities and mental health struggles, then became one of the first Special Educational Needs Organisers in Ireland, observing and providing school supports for students with atypical needs across 80 rural schools. While studying for a Master's degree in Autism, Joan met a variety of autistic adults, which led to her own autism assessment. Joan is passionate about using autistic students' interests to support learners of all levels of cognitive ability to access education.

Susanna Matthan

Susanna lives increasingly immersed in nature, contemplating and wandering through the seasons, capturing images of tiny things on her phone. She doodles, creates, makes and mends regularly. Despite struggling with the inadequacy of the written word to express herself, she has no shortage of thoughts, theories, ideas or emotions to keep her mind alive. Susanna accepts life as deep relational communion, staying present or radical as needed. She longs to travel, sometimes it's just down the road, but the woods, sea or the Arctic are often on her mind. She has a few treasured human and animal relationships. She is doing post-graduate study.

Andrew Miller

Andrew received a clinical autism diagnosis in 2019 at the age of 59 after having taught in mainstream and special schools across London for 30 years. His career in schools included senior leadership posts and he went on to become a local authority specialist autism advisory teacher. Andrew obtained a Master's degree in Autism and Children from the University of Birmingham. Having retired from teaching, he works as an independent autism education consultant, trainer and speaker. He is also the author of a book, *All About Me*, published by Jessica Kingsley Publishers, on how to tell autistic children and young people about their diagnosis.

Yasmeen Multani

Yasmeen Multani is a university lecturer and writes about the importance of ongoing mentorship for Autistic school staff. In 2020, she was awarded a Master of Arts in Special Educational Needs and Additional Learning Needs (Autism) with Distinction. Although no longer a classroom teacher, Yasmeen still has an avid interest in all matters relating to early childhood education. She is also passionate about pupil well-being and advocates for all neurodivergent people on Twitter on @wellbeingEyears. Yasmeen spends her spare time involved in self-care activities that include immersion in nature and Art in the form of make-up application. She is easily recognisable by her trademark 'red' lipstick.

Eiman Munro

Eiman Munro is a qualified Physics teacher and works as a Special Needs Teacher at a school run by the UK charity, the National Autistic Society. She was born in Baghdad, Iraq, and has also lived briefly in Syria and Iran but mainly resides in the UK. She enjoys processing the world through her journal and has been doing so since she was eight years old. Alongside teaching, she is writing children's stories and doing a Doctorate in Education at the University of East London.

Claire O'Neill

Claire is an autistic senior school leader in an Irish primary school. She is a qualified and experienced primary and secondary school teacher and has First Class Honours Postgraduate Diplomas in Special Education and Educational Leadership. She has recently been awarded a scholarship to study for a Master's of Education in Autism Studies. Claire is a Health and Wellbeing associate with the Professional Development Service for Teachers, facilitating training with teachers and school leaders. She also coaches neurodivergent adults. Coaching, Restorative Practices and Positive Education influence her leadership style. Claire lives with her autistic husband and two autistic children.

Sara Peeters

Sara is a photonics engineer with a Master's of Science degree. After being diagnosed autistic, she changed career to become a software developer and completed a degree in Computer Science. Sara loves creating things, be it writing software on her day job, sewing her own clothes in her free time, or drawing visual notes for everything. She implements illustration as a form of communication and understanding rather than as a fine art, and specialises in sketch-noting and graphic recording of talks, discussions and books.

Jade Ponnudurai

Jade is Autistic, dyslexic, dyspraxic and has Ehlers Danlos Syndrome. She has two degrees in Special and Inclusive Education and one degree in Fine Art. Jade worked in schools and colleges for five years before moving to a career in adult social care, working with Autistic adults. Outside of work, she volunteers with various charities and community interest projects. Her current hobby is dog training, as she is owner-training her assistance dog.

Kieran Rose

Kieran Rose was clinically diagnosed as Autistic in 2003 and is a parent of Autistic children. An international public speaker, Kieran provides specialist training aimed at reframing understanding of Autism. He offers private consultancy to organisations from all over the world and is academically published. Kieran's research specialises in Autistic masking, identity, monotropism and stigma. He is co-founder of a network for Autistic advocates, Senior Advisor to the therapist education organisation the Therapist Neurodiversity Collective, and is Neurodivergence Educator for the US-based Occupational Therapy charity, the Star Institute. His writing at www.theautisticadvocate.com has been read by over 1.5 million people.

Pete Wharmby

Pete Wharmby is a former English teacher of 13 years' experience who is now working in online tutoring and autism advocacy. He was diagnosed with autism in 2017 at the age of 34 and since then has worked hard to promote more accurate and positive information about autism to the general population. He is a keen writer, artist and musician and is the writer of two books about autism.

Madge Woollard

Madge has run her own business teaching piano and keyboard in schools and privately since 1994. She is a graduate of Cambridge University with a Bachelor of Arts Honours degree in music, and has a Post Graduate Certificate in Education in primary education. She was diagnosed autistic in 2016 at the age of 44. In 2019 she was awarded an Autism-Friendly Business Award from the National Autistic Society for her work teaching neurodivergent students. She lives in Sheffield with her wife, who is also late-diagnosed autistic.

Subject Index

Author Index